ROZ AULT

BASIC Programming for KIDS

BASIC Programming on Personal Computers by
APPLE
ATARI
COMMODORE
RADIO SHACK
TEXAS INSTRUMENTS
TIMEX SINCLAIR

Houghton Mifflin Company   Boston

To Mick, Mike, and Ben

Library of Congress Cataloging in Publication Data

Ault, Roz.
  BASIC programming for kids.

  Summary: A guide to programming the home computer in
BASIC emphasizing ways computers can be helpful and fun.
  1. Basic (Computer program language)—Juvenile
literature.   2. Microcomputers—Programming—Juvenile
literature.   [1. Basic (Computer program language)
2. Programming (Computers)   3. Microcomputers—Pro-
gramming]   I. Title.
QA76.73.B3A93   1983   001.64′24   83-12773
ISBN 0-395-34920-6

Printed in the United States of America

Q   10   9   8   7   6   5   4

Acknowledgments

This book really owes its conception to C. Michael and Michael C. Ault — the first for providing the wherewithal and the second for discovering the why and wherefore. In other words, it was my husband who had the idea to buy a computer in the first place and my son who was able to figure out what to do with it! This book couldn't have been written without their insights and collaboration.

Special recognition also should go to Ben Ault for his program ideas, and to the Hardy School parents, teachers, and children for the support, encouragement, and enthusiasm that made this project possible. Former teacher Nancy Gouveia deserves special mention for pointing the way to an elementary computer program in our schools. Other valuable input came from Tom Vaughn and his teaching teamwork. Thanks, too, to Frank Smith and Sheila and John Gill for the generous loans of their computers.

Finally, I want to acknowledge the influence of Russ Walter in this book's approach to computing. For me, Russ's publications (*The Secret Guide to Computers,* 92 St. Botolph Street, Boston, MA 02116) were the first to cut through the jargon and abstruseness that usually obscure this subject, proving that computers can be easy and fun for just about anybody.

Contents

Introduction

This is a book for children, parents, teachers — and anyone else who likes to learn. Its purpose is to help kids (and adults) to begin exploring an important and fascinating subject — computers.

A great deal has been said and written about the "computer revolution." It is here, and it is affecting all our lives in ways we don't even know about yet. The younger you are, the more impact computers will have on you — since you presumably have more years ahead to live in a world with more and more computers in it.

In order to use this book you should have (or have access to) a computer that "speaks" the computer language BASIC. (Every popular brand of general-purpose microcomputer now being sold for homes and schools uses BASIC.) This book will teach you how to write simple programs in BASIC for your computer. Its purpose, however, is not to make you a programmer. Its purpose is to help you understand computers, to think about how computers can help you in all kinds of ways, and to discover how much fun you can have when you learn how to talk to computers.

Here's where that old Chinese proverb holds true:

Tell me and I forget,
Show me and I remember,
Let me do, and I understand.

In acquiring knowledge and confidence about using computers, there is no substitute for doing — that is, learning how to write your own programs. They don't have to be long, involved, or complicated programs. In fact, after you've done a bit of programming, you may find it's not your thing and decide you'd rather just play computer games (or maybe go roller skating, or read a book). But once you've had that experience, your relation to the computer has changed. You no longer see it as a magical, mysterious machine you'd never think to question. And you'll be able to see more clearly why some programs work the way they do — and perhaps consider how they might work better.

The programs in these pages are only very simple examples of what you can do with a computer. But if you play around with them till you understand how they work, you'll have a pretty good foundation in communicating with a computer. If you then decide you want to learn more, there are plenty of other books and magazines to take you further. (And as with learning any language, it's easier to become really fluent if you start when you're young.) As you learn to make the computer work for you, you are gaining control over something that's right up there with the wheel — one of the most powerful tools human beings have ever invented.

1. All Keyed Up

In this chapter you will be learning about the keyboard on your computer. At the time this book is being written, the most common computers for homes and schools are:

🍎	*Apple II+ or IIe*	**TI**	*Texas Instruments 99/4A*
𝘈	*ATARI 400 or 800*	**T/S**	*Timex/Sinclair 1000*
C=	*Commodore* (*VIC 20, 64, or PET*)	**TRS**	*TRS-80 (Model I, III, and Color)*

If you have one of these computers, you'll find specific instructions for your machine in this book. But you should be able to use this book with just about any personal computer. The examples will work pretty much the same way on all types of machines. Just keep your manual handy in case you get stumped about which keys to press to make something happen.

Before you can really start talking to your computer, you'll have to figure out how to get your messages out of your head and into the machine. Since your computer can't understand speech, you'll have to let your fingers do the talking. (Or in computer jargon, you must learn to *input* information from the keyboard.)

The letters on all of these computer keyboards are just like the letters on a typewriter. But each computer has several special keys, or combinations of keys, that make it work in special ways. This chapter will explain how to use

1

these keys to type words and numbers (and on some computers, pictures). It will show you how certain keys can make the computer do some fancy tricks.

Once you know how to use the keys, then you can get started on learning the language. The most important key to using the computer, though, isn't on the keyboard — it's inside you. Your ideas make the computer work. So any time you have an idea — try it out. That's what your computer is for: it's a machine for you to think with. Explore, experiment, express yourself — and above all, have fun! Remember — there's no way you can hurt the computer by typing on it.

This book is here to help you acquire a few skills you'll need to make your computer work for you. Use it only as a guide — a starting point for your own imagination.

To begin, turn to the section that describes your computer's keyboard. The instructions you'll find there are your jumping-off place for communicating with your computer.

If you have a computer that is not one of the six listed above, turn to the Practice section at the end of Chapter 1. When you can answer those questions for your computer, then go on to Chapter 2.

Apple Keyboard

1. Turn It On.

Make sure everything is plugged in. Find the switch (on the Apple, it's on the back) and flick it on. Turn on the TV set or monitor. Turn the volume all the way down if you are using a television set.

If you have a disk drive and are not using a disk, you will probably have to hold down the key marked CTRL or CONTROL (on the left side) and press the RESET key (upper right) in order to get started.

If you are using an Apple IIe, make sure the CAPS LOCK key is pressed down.

2. The Cursor.

Somewhere at the left side of the screen you should see a flashing square or box. This is called the *cursor*. The cursor shows you where your typing will appear on the screen.

You should also see a square bracket called a *prompt* to the left of the cursor. The square bracket tells you the computer is ready to use the Apple's version of the BASIC language, known as Applesoft. If you don't see the square bracket, check your manual to find out how to get into Applesoft.

Press the long key at the bottom of the keyboard. This is called the *space bar*. Notice how the space bar moves the cursor one space to the right every time you press it.

3. Fixing Your Mistakes.

Typing letters on the computer keyboard is just like typing on a typewriter. But it's easier to correct your mistakes on the computer.

Type your first name. Press the space bar. Then type your last name.

Press the key that looks like this $\boxed{\leftarrow}$. Press it again. Notice how the cursor backs up. When you want to change a letter, use this left arrow key to move the cursor to the mistake. Then type the correction. If you want to erase something instead of changing it, move the cursor back, then erase with the space bar. After you have made your correction, you can use the right arrow key $\boxed{\rightarrow}$ to move the cursor to the right without erasing anything.

Practice. Type this word: CUMPUTER. Do you see the spelling mistake? Back up the cursor and correct the word to spell COMPUTER.

4. Confusing the Computer.

Type your name. Press the key marked $\boxed{\text{RETURN}}$. What words appear on the screen?

You should see the message SYNTAX ERROR. That means that the computer does not understand you. Your name is not a word in the computer's language.

Pressing the $\boxed{\text{RETURN}}$ key means, to the computer, that you have just finished giving it some information. If the computer does not understand the information, it will give back the message SYNTAX ERROR, which means "wrong word." Any error message is only the computer's way of saying "what did you mean?" or "I'm confused." It does *not* mean you've done anything to hurt the computer.

5. Shift Keys.

Type the number 4 on the top row of keys. Now find a $\boxed{\text{SHIFT}}$ key. (There are two $\boxed{\text{SHIFT}}$ keys. You may use either one.) Put one finger on a $\boxed{\text{SHIFT}}$ key. While you are holding down the $\boxed{\text{SHIFT}}$ key with one hand, type 4 again with the other hand. What appears on the screen? (You should get a dollar sign: $.)

Keep holding the $\boxed{\text{SHIFT}}$ key and type the number 5. What appears? (You should get a percentage sign: %.) Can you explain what the $\boxed{\text{SHIFT}}$ key does when you type a number? What do you think you will get if you type the $\boxed{\text{SHIFT}}$ key and the number 8? Try it.

6. Clearing the Screen.

You know how to erase letters on the screen one at a time. Now let's erase the whole screen at once. Here's how:

First type a few lines of letters. Then press the $\boxed{\text{ESC}}$ key, hold down the $\boxed{\text{SHIFT}}$ key, and type @. (On the II+ the @ sign is on the P; on the IIe it's on the 2.) Presto — everything disappears! (You may also clear the screen by typing the word HOME and pressing $\boxed{\text{RETURN}}$. If this doesn't work the first time, press $\boxed{\text{RETURN}}$ and try again.)

7. Letters and Numbers.

Type the letter O. (It is between I and P in the second row.) Type the zero. (It is next to the 9 in the top row.)

Do you see the difference between the computer letter O and zero? It's important to remember that the computer makes a zero with a slash through it.

Type the letter I (second row, next to U).

Type the letter L (third row, next to K).

Type the number 1 (top row, next to 2).

Type the word OIL. Type the number 1001. Look hard at these as they appear on the screen. Computers get very confused if you mix up your letters and numbers. So remember to keep them straight! Any time you mean to type a number, it must be one of the keys in the top row.

Special Keys: Apple II+ and IIe

This section gives you a quick run-down on the keys that perform special functions. It will tell you all you need to know to get started. For a more advanced discussion, consult your Apple manual.

1. The Control Key.

The CTRL or CONTROL key is on the left side of the keyboard. When you press the CONTROL key followed by a letter, you are typing a *control* character. Usually this means nothing will appear on the screen. Try this. Start with the letter A and move to the right across the keyboard, pressing CTRL or CONTROL before each letter, like this:

CONTROL A CONTROL S CONTROL D CONTROL F CONTROL G

What happened when you got to G? You should have heard the Apple beep at you. (That's the same sound you'll hear when you make a SYNTAX ERROR or some other move that makes the Apple want to get your attention.) But before that you shouldn't have seen or heard anything happen.

The CONTROL key sends "secret" messages to the computer which you usually can't see. Sometimes if you accidentally type CONTROL the computer will get a confusing message that you don't even know you're sending. Then it might tell you SYNTAX ERROR even though you can't see any problem in what you typed. In that case your best bet is just to retype the line.

One way you can use the CONTROL key is with X. Typing CONTROL X will make the computer print a backslash and jump the cursor to the next line. It tells the computer "Ignore this line." Try this: Type your name and press RETURN. You get a beep and a SYNTAX ERROR. Then type your name, CONTROL X, and RETURN. There is no syntax error because the CONTROL X told the computer to forget what you just typed. CONTROL X is useful if you type something, then change your mind.

Another key you will often use with CONTROL is C. CONTROL C tells the computer "Stop!" It's explained in Chapter 3.

2. The Repeat Function.

Suppose you want to make the computer type a whole row of A's. On the IIe all you have to do is press down the A (or any other key you want to repeat) and keep holding it. On the II+ you must hold down the REPT key (on the right side of the keyboard) while you press the A (or any other key).

The repeat function is especially useful with the left and right arrow keys, as it lets you move the cursor quickly backward and forward.

3. ESC Stands for *Escape*.

The ESC key is on the left side of the keyboard. Pressing the ESC key with certain other keys lets you ESCape to different places on the screen. You've already learned how to clear the screen with ESC SHIFT @. Here are some other ways to use ESC:

        ESC A or ESC K moves the cursor right
        ESC B or ESC J moves the cursor left
        ESC C or ESC M moves the cursor down
        ESC D or ESC I moves the cursor up

ESC E erases everything on the same line to the right of the cursor

ESC F erases everything from the cursor to the end of the screen

[ESC] I, J, K, M also put the Apple in Edit mode. If you want to read more about that, see the section on editing in the back of this book (Appendix III) or check your Apple manual.

4. RESET Means *Stop.*

The [RESET] key is on the upper right side of the keyboard. When you press the [RESET] key, you're telling the Apple: "Stop what you're doing, I want to start over again." Pressing [RESET] also creates a beep.

On the IIe you must hold the [CONTROL] key while you press [RESET]. (Sometimes you need to press the "open-Apple" key, as well. See Section 5, just below.)

On the II+ it may be possible to stop the computer by pressing the [RESET] key alone. Since the [RESET] key is so close to the [RETURN] key on the II+, it's easy to press it accidentally, which can get to be a real nuisance. Therefore, if you haven't already done so, you should fix the [RESET] key so it works only in combination with [CTRL]. You can do this with the little switch just inside the keyboard. (Ask your dealer to show you where it is if you don't know.)

5. The Apple Keys.

On the IIe there are two keys with the Apple design, one on each side of the space bar. The "open-Apple" key is on the left; the "closed-Apple" is on the right.

The open-Apple key, when pressed with [CONTROL] and [RESET], lets you stop a program and start over.

Both Apple keys may be used in games and other special programs. They are called *function keys*, because they may have different functions in different programs. For this book you won't need them.

If you are using an Apple computer, now skip to the Practice section at the end of Chapter 1.

Atari Keyboard

1. Turn It On.

Make sure everything is plugged in and that the BASIC cartridge is in the machine. Find the switch and flick it on. Turn on the TV monitor. Turn the volume all the way down on the TV.

2. The Cursor.

Somewhere at the left side of the screen you should see a little square or box. This is called the *cursor*. The cursor shows you where your typing will appear on the screen.

   Press the long key at the bottom of the keyboard. This is called the *space bar*. Notice how the space bar moves the cursor one space to the right every time you press it.

3. Fixing Your Mistakes.

Typing letters on the computer keyboard is just like typing on a typewriter. But it's easier to correct your mistakes on the computer.

   Type your first name. Press the space bar. Then type your last name. Now press the DELETE/BACK S key to move the cursor to the left. Notice how it erases the letters as it moves. This is the key to use when you want to correct a mistake.

Practice. Type this word: CUMPUTER. Do you see the spelling mistake? Back up the cursor and correct the word to spell COMPUTER.

4. Confusing the Computer.

Type your name. Press the key marked RETURN. What words appear on the screen?

   You should get the message ERROR — followed by your name. That means that the computer does not understand you. Your name is not a word in the computer's language.

Pressing the RETURN key means, to the computer, that you have just finished giving it some information. If the computer does not understand the information, it will give you an ERROR message. An error message does *not* mean you have hurt the computer. It only means the computer is confused.

5. Shift Keys.

Type the number 4 on the top row of keys. Now find a SHIFT key. (There are two SHIFT keys. You may use either one.) Put one finger on a SHIFT key. While you are holding down the SHIFT key with one hand, type 4 again with the other hand. What appears on the screen? (You should get a dollar sign: $.) Keep holding the SHIFT key and type the number 5. What appears? (You should get a percentage sign: %.)

Can you explain what the SHIFT key does when you type a number? What do you think you will get if you type the SHIFT key and the number 8? Try it.

Type a few letters. Now hold down the SHIFT key and press DELETE/BACK S . The whole line should disappear.

6. Clearing the Screen.

You know how to erase one letter at a time and one whole line at a time. Now let's erase the whole screen at once. Here's how:

First type several lines of anything you want. Then hold down the SHIFT key, and press CLEAR/ < . Presto — everything disappears! (If this doesn't work the first time, press RETURN and try again.)

7. Letters and Numbers.

Type the letter O. (It is between I and P in the second row.) Type zero. (It is next to the 9 in the top row.)

Do you see the difference between the computer letter O and zero? On the

Atari the zero has a wiggly line through the center. Many other computers print a zero with a slash through it, like this Ø. That is the way we'll show a zero in this book, to distinguish it from the letter O.

Type the letter I (second row, next to U).

Type the letter L (third row, next to K).

Type the number 1 (top row, next to 2).

Type the word OIL. Type the number 1ØØ1. Look hard at these as they appear on the screen. Computers get very confused if you mix up your letters and numbers. So remember to keep them straight! Any time you mean to type a number, it must be one of the keys in the top row.

Special Keys: Atari

[SHIFT], [CTRL], and [ESC] are three keys that don't do anything by themselves. Their job is to make certain other keys behave in different ways.

We've already seen how to use the [SHIFT] key to get the special symbols over the numbers, to clear the screen (with [CLEAR/ <]), and to erase a line (with [DELETE/BACK S]).

1. The CTRL Key.

The [CTRL] (for CONTROL) key, when pressed along with any letter, puts special graphics characters on the screen. For example, hold [CTRL] and press the comma. You should see a little heart. Experiment with other keys to see what special pictures you can get. (Check the Atari manual for a list of these.)

The [CTRL] key is also used with the four arrow keys on the right side of the keyboard to move the cursor around the screen without erasing anything. For example, if you want to move the cursor up one line, hold down [CTRL] and type [↑–].

Press [CTRL] 2 to hear the Atari sound its buzzer. [CTRL] [CLEAR/ <] will clear the screen just like [SHIFT] [CLEAR/ <].

2. The ESC Key.

The $\boxed{\text{ESC}}$ (for ESCAPE) key is used mainly in programs to carry out certain commands. (For example, PRINT "$\boxed{\text{ESC}}$ $\boxed{\text{CTRL}}$ $\boxed{\text{CLEAR}}$" is one way of clearing the screen.) Typing $\boxed{\text{ESC}}$ with certain other special function keys prints special graphics characters on the screen. Refer to the Atari manual for a full list.

3. A Change of Scene.

Pressing the ⅄ key (say "the Atari key") or the $\boxed{\text{CAPS/LOWR}}$ key changes the way your typing looks on the screen. The Atari key ⅄ reverses your typing from light to dark and back again.

4. Upper and Lower.

When you press the $\boxed{\text{CAPS/LOWR}}$ key once, the letters on the screen will change from capitals to small letters. To go back to upper case, hold the $\boxed{\text{SHIFT}}$ key and type $\boxed{\text{CAPS/LOWR}}$ again.

5. CLR/SET/TAB: A Key for Spacing.

Pressing the $\boxed{\text{CLR/SET/TAB}}$ key alone makes the cursor jump over 8 spaces. You can change the number of spaces it jumps in one move by pressing $\boxed{\text{SHIFT}}$ and $\boxed{\text{CLR/SET/TAB}}$. The computer will then set a tab stop wherever the cursor happens to be on the line. To clear the tab you've just set, press $\boxed{\text{CLR/SET/TAB}}$ with $\boxed{\text{CTRL}}$.

6. Insert and Delete.

To insert or erase one character, press $\boxed{\text{INSERT}}$ or $\boxed{\text{DELETE}}$ with $\boxed{\text{CTRL}}$. To insert or delete a whole line, press $\boxed{\text{INSERT}}$ or $\boxed{\text{DELETE}}$ with $\boxed{\text{SHIFT}}$.

7. Repeating Function.

Any key on the Atari will start to repeat itself (print over and over again) if you hold it down for more than half a second.

If you are using an Atari, now skip to the Practice section at the end of Chapter 1.

Commodore Keyboard

1. Turn It On.

Make sure everything is plugged in. Find the switch and flick it on. If your computer is attached to a separate TV set or monitor, turn on the TV. Turn the volume all the way down on the TV.

2. The Cursor.

Somewhere at the left side of the screen you should see a flashing square or box. This is called the *cursor.* The cursor shows you where your typing will appear on the screen.

Press the long key at the bottom of the keyboard. This is called the *space bar.* Notice how the space bar moves the cursor one space to the right every time you press it.

3. Fixing Your Mistakes.

Typing letters on the computer keyboard is just like typing on a typewriter. But it's easier to correct your mistakes on the computer.

Type your first name. Press the space bar. Then type your last name. Press the key marked INST/DEL . (This stands for Insert/Delete.) Press it again. Notice how it erases the letters. This is the key you use to correct a mistake.
Practice. Type this word: CUMPUTER. Do you see the spelling mistake? Back up the cursor and correct the word to spell COMPUTER.

4. Confusing the Computer.

Type your name. Press the key marked RETURN. What words appear on the screen?

You should get the message SYNTAX ERROR. That means that the computer does not understand you. Your name is not a word in the computer's language.

Pressing the RETURN key means, to the computer, that you have just finished giving it some information. If the computer does not understand the information, it will give back the message SYNTAX ERROR, which means "wrong word." An error message does *not* mean you have hurt the computer. It only means that the computer is confused.

5. Shift Keys.

(*Note:* For the PET only, skip to the special exception below.) Type the number 4 on the top row of keys. Now find a SHIFT key. (On most computers there are two SHIFT keys. You may use either one.) Put one finger on a SHIFT key. While you are holding down the SHIFT key with one hand, type 4 again with the other hand. What appears on the screen? (You should get a dollar sign: $.) Keep holding the SHIFT key and type the number 5. What appears? (You should get a percentage sign: %.)

Can you explain what the SHIFT key does when you type a number? What do you think you will get if you type the SHIFT key and the number 8? Try it. *Exception for PET:* The number keys on the PET are along the right-hand side of the keyboard. When you type the SHIFT key on the PET you get one of the special graphics symbols that appear on each letter or number key. (For more about the special graphic symbols on Commodore computers see Special Keys: Commodore.)

6. Clearing the Screen.

You know how to erase letters on the screen one at a time. Now let's erase the whole screen at once. Here's how:

Hold down the SHIFT key and press CLR/HOME . (If this doesn't work the first time, press RETURN and try again.)

7. Letters and Numbers.

Type the letter O. (It is between I and P in the second row.) Type zero. (On the VIC keyboard, it is next to the 9 in the top row. On the PET keyboard it's on the right, with the numbers.)

Do you see the difference between the computer letter O and zero? It's important to remember that the computer makes a zero with a slash through it.

Type the letter I (second row, next to U).

Type the letter L (third row, next to K).

Type the number 1 (top row, next to 2).

Type the word OIL. Type the number 1001. Look hard at these as they appear on the screen. Computers get very confused if you mix up your letters and numbers. So remember to keep them straight! Any time you mean to type a number, it must be one of the keys in the top row. (Or for the PET, it must be one of the keys on the right-hand side.)

Special Keys: Commodore

Note: The VIC 20 and Commodore 64 have identical keyboards with several special keys. The PET keyboard is a little different. For PET users: See the special note at the end of this section.

1. Graphic Symbols with Shift.

On the front of the letters on the VIC keyboard you will notice two different sets of symbols. Here's how to type those graphic characters.

Type the letter S. Hold down the SHIFT key and type S again. You should get a heart. Keep holding the SHIFT key and type Q. What do you get? (This is supposed to be a circle, but computers don't draw circles very well.)

You will see that the SHIFT key lets you type the characters on the right side of the front of the letter keys. Experiment with using the SHIFT key to type other characters.

2. Graphics Symbols with the Commodore Key.

Now hold down the key marked C= (this is called the Commodore key) and type S. What appears? Keep holding the Commodore key and type B. What do you get? Notice how the Commodore key gives you the symbols on the left side of the key.

3. Shift Lock.

Push the SHIFT/LOCK key and let go. (It should stay pressed down even though you are not holding it.)

Type 1 2 3. What do you get? Type Q W E. What appears? Notice that the SHIFT/LOCK key works just like the SHIFT key, but you don't have to keep holding it down. To release the SHIFT/LOCK key, tap it again lightly.

4. Upper and Lower Case.

Type your name. Now press the SHIFT and the Commodore C= key at the same time. What happens to the capital letters? You have just changed from upper-case mode to lower-case mode. Type a few letters — they should appear as small letters. Then hold the SHIFT key down and type a few more letters. They should come out as capital letters.

Now press the SHIFT and Commodore C= keys together again to go back to regular upper-case mode. Observe how the capital letters change into the graphic symbols.

Notice that you can have *either* capital letters and small letters *or* capital letters and the graphic character on the right side of the keyboard. You cannot type the right-side graphic symbols, such as the heart, with small letters. (You can, however, type the left-hand symbols, which you get with the Commodore key, along with the small letters.)

5. Moving the Cursor.

Experiment with the two keys on the right marked CRSR and CRSR . Type them with and without the SHIFT key. Notice how you can make the cursor move around the screen without erasing anything. You can use these keys to move the cursor when you want to make a correction without wiping out your other typing. (For more information see Appendix III: Editing Your Mistakes.)

6. Changing Colors.

If you have a color TV, experiment with changing colors by typing the CTRL key and the keys from 1 through 8. You must hold down the CTRL key while you type the color key. If you have a black and white TV, you will notice a slight change in the shading, but of course you won't be able to get different colors on the screen. (Incidentally, if you're wondering about the color CYN, that stands for cyan, which is a shade of blue.)

Hold down the CTRL key and type 9. That gives you REVERSE ON (which means you get white letters on a dark background). To go back to normal, hold down CTRL and type Ø.

7. Repeating Keys.

Some of the keys on the VIC are repeating keys. If you press them and keep holding them down, they will keep on going. For example, the space bar, the INST/DEL , and the two cursor arrow keys can repeat. Hold any of them down and see what happens.

8. Function Keys.

Don't worry about the four keys labeled F1 through F8 on the right side of the keyboard. In some games or other types of programs they are given special functions to perform, but you won't need to use them for anything in this book.

9. Restore Key.

The RESTORE key is used with RUN/STOP to make the computer stop a program. This is demonstrated in Chapter 4, Section 8.

Special Note for PET computers: You can get graphics characters on the PET with the SHIFT key (Section 1 above) and you can move the cursor with the cursor arrow keys (Section 5). The PET does not have the other special keys of the VIC keyboard, and it does not have color. You can reverse the letters (from light to dark) using the OFF/RVS key. To go back to normal press SHIFT with OFF/RVS.

If you have a "business style" keyboard (found on CBM computers) the normal mode of typing is upper and lower case. To get the graphics characters instead of lower case letters type this: POKE 59468, 12 RETURN. When you want to go back to upper and lower case type POKE 59468, 14 RETURN.

If you are using a Commodore, now skip to the Practice section at the end of Chapter 1.

TRS-80 Keyboard

1. Turn It On.

Make sure everything is plugged in. Find the switch and flick it on. If your computer is attached to a separate TV set or monitor, turn on the TV. Turn the volume all the way down on the TV.

You are ready to start typing when you see the word READY (or, on the Color Computer, OK) on the screen. If you don't see READY, press the ENTER key until it appears.

If you have a TRS-80 with a disk drive and you can't get the computer going, try this: Hold down the BREAK key and press the orange reset key on the right side of the keyboard. Do this several times if necessary. You may also need to adjust the tuning on the TV screen with the controls under the left side of the keyboard.

2. The Cursor.

Somewhere at the left side of the screen you should see a little square or box (or on the Model I, just a little line). This is called the *cursor.* The cursor shows you where your typing will appear on the screen.

You should also see a *prompt* to the left of the cursor. It looks like a sideways V: >. The prompt tells you when you're beginning a new line.

Press the long key at the bottom of the keyboard. This is called the *space bar.* Notice how the space bar moves the cursor one space to the right every time you press it.

3. Fixing Your Mistakes.

Typing letters on the computer keyboard is just like typing on a typewriter. But it's easier to correct your mistakes on the computer.

Type your first name. Press the space bar. Then type your last name. Press the left arrow key ⬅. Notice how it moves the cursor back and erases the letters as it goes. Use this key to back up and make a correction when you make a mistake. .

Practice: Type this word: CUMPUTER. Do you see the spelling mistake? Back up the cursor and correct the word to spell COMPUTER.

4. Confusing the Computer.

Type your name. Press the key marked ENTER. What words appear on the screen?

You should get the message SN ERROR, which is an abbreviation for SYN-TAX ERROR. That means that the computer does not understand you. Your name is not a word in the computer's language.

Pressing the ENTER key means, to the computer, that you have just finished giving it some information. If the computer does not understand the information, it will give back the message SYNTAX ERROR, which means "wrong word." An error message does *not* mean you have hurt the computer. It only means that the computer is confused.

5. Shift Keys.

Type the number 4 on the top row of keys. Now find a SHIFT key. (On most computers there are two SHIFT keys. You may use either one.) Put one finger on a SHIFT key. While you are holding down the SHIFT key with one hand, type 4 again with the other hand. What appears on the screen? (You should get a dollar sign: $.) Keep holding the SHIFT key and type the number 5. What appears? (You should get a percentage sign: %.)

Can you explain what the SHIFT key does when you type a number? What do you think you will get if you type the SHIFT key and the number 8? Try it.

Now type a whole line of letters. Then hold SHIFT and press the left arrow key. Notice how SHIFT ← erases the whole line.

6. Clearing the Screen.

You know how to erase letters on the screen one at a time with the left arrow key and how to erase a whole line at a time with SHIFT and the left arrow. Now let's erase the whole screen at once. Here's how:

First type several lines of anything. Then just press the CLEAR key. Presto — it's all gone!

7. Letters and Numbers.

Type the letter O. (It is between I and P in the second row.) Type zero. (It is next to the 9 in the top row.)

Do you see the difference between the computer letter O and zero? It's important to remember that the computer makes a zero with a slash through it.

Type the letter I (second row, next to U).

Type the letter L (third row, next to K).

Type the number 1 (top row, next to 2).

Type the word OIL. Type the number 1Ø01. Look hard at these as they appear on the screen. Computers get very confused if you mix up your letters and numbers. So remember to keep them straight! Any time you mean to type a number, it must be one of the keys in the top row. (Or if your computer has a special set of number keys like a calculator, those are okay too.)

Special Keys: TRS-80

The TRS-80 has four arrow keys, pointing left, right, up, and down. You've already seen how to use the left arrow key to erase one letter at a time, and how to use the left arrow key with SHIFT to erase a whole line at a time. Each of the other arrow keys does something a little different. Experiment with them so you understand how they work.

1. Right Arrow Key.

The right arrow key → makes the cursor skip forward 8 spaces. The right arrow key when used with SHIFT on Models I and III does something very unexpected. Try this. Type HHEELLLLOO. Now hold the SHIFT key and press the →. You should see a big HELLO.

Pressing SHIFT → makes the letters twice as wide as normal. Anything you type now will appear in double-size letters. But anything you've already typed will lose every other letter. To get back to normal size press CLEAR.

2. The Down Arrow Key.

The down arrow key ↓, as you might expect, makes the cursor skip down to the next line on the screen.

3. The Up Arrow Key.

The left arrow key ← moves the cursor left. The right arrow key → moves the cursor right. And the down arrow key ↓ moves the cursor down. But the up arrow key ⬚↑ — instead of doing what you might expect — does *not* move the cursor up. Instead, it prints something on the screen. Depending on which model TRS-80 you have it may print an arrow ↑, or it may print a square bracket [. (Actually, this is an exponent key. You use this when you want to type something like 10 to the third power. Math books sometimes write this as 10^3. On the computer you type it 10↑3.)

4. Shift and Zero.

One other combination of keys you should know about is SHIFT Ø. On some models of the TRS-80, typing those two together will put you in lower-case mode. When that happens, every letter you type will come out as a small letter. If you want a capital letter, you have to use the SHIFT key (just like a regular typewriter.) To go back to normal upper-case mode press SHIFT Ø again.

On the TRS-80 Color Computer SHIFT Ø makes the letters on the screen go into reverse mode printing — instead of black on green, they become green on black. In reverse mode the computer will not carry out your commands the way it does normally — so you should stick to the regular letters for writing your programs. Typing SHIFT Ø again will put the computer back in normal mode.

If you are using a TRS-80, now skip to the Practice section at the end of Chapter 1.

Texas Instruments Keyboard

1. Turn It On.

Make sure everything is plugged in. Find the switch and flick it on. Turn on the TV set, or monitor, and follow the instructions on the screen to start up TI BASIC.

2. The Cursor.

At the bottom left side of the screen you should see a little flashing box. This is called the *cursor*. The cursor shows you where your typing will appear on the screen.

You should also see a *prompt* to the left of the cursor. It looks like a sideways V: >. The prompt tells you when you're beginning a new line.

Press the long key at the bottom of the keyboard. This is called the *space bar*. Notice how the space bar moves the cursor one space to the right every time you press it.

3. Typing Letters — Large and Small.

Typing letters on the computer keyboard is just like typing on a typewriter.

Type your first name. Press the space bar. Press the ALPHA LOCK key. (Or if the ALPHA LOCK key was already pressed when you started typing, then press it again to release it.) Now type your last name. Notice that the ALPHA LOCK key gives you bigger capital letters. If you find the larger letters easier to read, you'll probably want to leave the ALPHA LOCK key pressed down for all your typing.

4. Fixing Mistakes.

With your right hand hold down the key marked FCTN at the lower right. While holding FCTN, press S (the key with a left arrow ← on its front). Notice how the cursor backs up. When you want to change a letter, use FCTN S to move the cursor to the mistake. Then type the correction. If you want to erase a letter instead of changing it, move the cursor back and then erase with the space bar. When you have made the correction, you can use FCTN D (the right arrow) to move the cursor back to the right without erasing anything.

Put the cursor back at the end of your name. Now hold the FCTN key and press 3. Your name (and anything else on that line) disappears! FCTN 3 erases a whole line of typing with two keystrokes.

Practice. Type this word: CUMPUTER. Do you see the spelling mistake? Back up the cursor and correct the word to spell COMPUTER.

5. Confusing the Computer.

Type your name. Press the key marked [ENTER]. What words appear on the screen?

You should get the message INCORRECT STATEMENT. That means that the computer does not understand you. Your name is not a word in the computer's language.

Pressing the [ENTER] key means, to the computer, that you have just finished giving it some information. If the computer does not understand the information, it tells you that you made an INCORRECT STATEMENT. (On most other computers, this message would be SYNTAX ERROR.) A message like this does *not* mean you have hurt the computer. It only means that the computer is confused.

6. Shift Keys.

Type the number 4 on the top row of keys. Now find a [SHIFT] key. Put one finger on a [SHIFT] key. While you are holding down the [SHIFT] key with one hand, type 4 again with the other hand. What appears on the screen? (You should get a dollar sign: $.) Keep holding the [SHIFT] key and type the number 5. What appears? (You should get a percentage sign: %.)

Can you explain what the [SHIFT] key does when you type a number? What do you think you will get if you type the [SHIFT] key and the number 8? Try it. *Note:* If the [ALPHA LOCK] key is not pressed, holding the [SHIFT] key will also give you large capitals when you type letters.

7. Clearing the Screen.

You know how to erase letters on the screen one at a time with [FCTN] S and the space bar, and how to erase a whole line at a time with [FCTN] 3. Now let's erase the whole screen at once. Here's how:

First type several lines of anything. Then press ENTER (and just ignore the INCORRECT STATEMENT), type the words CALL CLEAR and press the ENTER key. Presto — it's all gone! (If this doesn't work the first time, press ENTER and try again.)

8. Letters and Numbers.

Type the letter O. (It is between I and P in the second row.) Type zero. (It is next to the 9 in the top row.)

Do you see the difference between the computer letter O and zero? Notice that on the TI the zero is more oval-shaped and the letter O is a rectangle. (On most other computers, however, a zero appears on the screen with a slash through it, the way it looks on the TI keyboard.)

Type the letter I (second row, next to U).

Type the letter L (third row, next to K).

Type the number 1 (top row, next to 2).

Type the word OIL. Type the number 1001. Look hard at these as they appear on the screen. Computers get very confused if you mix up your letters and numbers. So remember to keep them straight! Any time you mean to type a number, it must be one of the keys in the top row.

9. More Functions.

You've seen how to use the FCTN (for FUNCTION) key to move the cursor (with S and D) and to erase a whole line (with 3). The FCTN key also allows you to type any of the special symbols on the front of some of the letter keys. (One that's very important is the quotation mark on the front of the P.) Experiment with typing FCTN and the letter keys to see those symbols.

FCTN 1 and FCTN 2 are used in editing or correcting. For an explanation of how to use these, see Appendix III: Editing Your Mistakes (at the back of the book).

You won't need to use most of the other special functions any time soon. But one to watch out for is FCTN ±. Press that now to see what happens. If you ever press FCTN ± by mistake (and it isn't hard to do), you'll wipe out everything that is in the computer's memory at that moment. So be careful!

CTRL stands for CONTROL, but the special functions of this key are for advanced programmers. You won't need to worry about them now.

If you are using a Texas Instruments computer, now skip to the Practice section at the end of Chapter 1.

Timex Sinclair Keyboard

1. Turn It On.

There is no on-off switch on the Timex Sinclair. When everything is plugged in correctly, the computer will come on. Make sure the TV is on and the volume is turned all the way down.

2. The Cursor.

The cursor is a small box that shows you where your typing will appear on the screen. When you first turn on the Timex Sinclair, the cursor appears with the letter K inside it. This stands for Keyword. When you see the K cursor, your keyboard will not type letters like a typewriter. Instead, the next time you press a letter, you will get the keyword that is printed in small letters just above the letter. You'll learn more about what those keywords mean in later chapters.

For now we're just experimenting with the keyboard, so press P. The word PRINT should appear on the screen. Notice that the K in the cursor has now changed into an L. That stands for Letter, and means that the next time you press a key the letter (not the keyword) will appear on the screen. To check this, type your first name. Press the space key and type your last name.

3. Fixing Your Mistakes.

Here's what to do if you make a typing mistake. Hold down the SHIFT key (at the lower right). Press 5 while holding SHIFT. Notice that the cursor moves to the left and opens up a space wherever it stops. When you want to make a correction, you must first back up the cursor with SHIFT 5. If you want to erase a letter, you put the cursor right after the letter and type SHIFT Ø.

Practice. Type this word: CUMPUTR. Now let's correct it to spell COMPUTER. Follow these steps:

1. First back up the cursor between the T and R. Type E.
2. Now back up again (with SHIFT 5) till the cursor is between the U and the M.
3. Hold SHIFT and press Ø (zero). That erases the U. Now type the letter O to spell the word correctly.
4. To move the cursor back to the right, press SHIFT 8.

4. More About Shifting.

Notice that any time you press a key while holding the SHIFT key you will get whatever is printed in red on that key. For example, SHIFT 1 will print AND. SHIFT P prints quotation marks.

Practice. First, erase anything you have typed, using SHIFT Ø. Then experiment with using the SHIFT key while typing other keys.

5. Clearing the Screen.

What you are typing on the Timex Sinclair always appears at the bottom of the screen. But when you finish typing an instruction, the Timex Sinclair carries out the directions at the top of the screen.

Try this: Press P (for PRINT) and type the first 8 numbers: 12345678. Press ENTER, and the numbers appear at the top of the screen. To get rid of them, press V. This is the CLS (for Clear Screen) key — and it erases anything on the TV screen. (The Ø/Ø that appears at the bottom of the screen is a code message. When the first number is zero, it means everything is okay. You can look up the meaning of those code messages in the back of your Timex Sinclair manual.)

6. Confusing the Computer.

Press A, which puts the word NEW on the screen. Then type your name. Press [ENTER]. What happens?

You should see an S in a black box appear. That S stands for SYNTAX ERROR, which means you've given the computer some confusing instructions. [ENTER], to the computer, means you have just finished sending it a message. But your name is not a word the computer understands. So it complains, with a SYNTAX ERROR message. In order to stop the computer's complaint, erase the line with [SHIFT] Ø.

7. Letters and Numbers.

Be sure you notice the difference between the computer letter O and Ø. It's important to remember that the computer makes a zero with a slash through it.

Also, don't get the number 1 and the letter I confused. They may look alike when you write them, but they mean two very different things to the computer. Any time you mean to type a number, it must be one of the keys in the top row.

8. Printing Graphics.

To print the graphics symbols on the keys, do this: Hold the [SHIFT] key and press 9. The cursor letter should change to G. Then keep holding the [SHIFT] key and type QWERTY. A checkered pattern should appear. To get back to normal, press [SHIFT] 9 again.

9. Function Keys.

To print the words that appear under each key, hold SHIFT and press ENTER. This changes the cursor to **F** (for Function). Now when you press **P**, for instance, you will see the word **TAB** appear. We'll be using a couple of these functions later in programs, but you don't have to worry about them for now.

Practice 1

After you have completed Chapter 1, check yourself with these questions.

1. What key (or keys) do you push to erase a letter you have just typed, or to correct a mistake?
2. What is the cursor?
3. What do you type to get an exclamation point (!)?
4. How do you clear the screen (that is, erase everything on the screen)?
5. What does the long key at the bottom of the keyboard do?
6. What are the words the computer tells you when it doesn't understand you?
7. How does the computer make a zero?

Answers to Practice 1

1. Apple — Left arrow key
   Atari — DELETE/BACK S
   Commodore — INST/DEL
   TRS-80 — Left arrow key
   Texas Instruments — FCTN S
   Timex Sinclair — SHIFT Ø
2. The little box or other marker that shows where your typing will appear on the screen.

3. On most computers, $\boxed{\text{SHIFT}}$ and 1. (Exceptions: On the PET, you type only the key with the ! on it. On the Timex Sinclair there is no exclamation point.)

4. Apple — $\boxed{\text{ESC}}$ $\boxed{\text{SHIFT}}$ @

   Atari — $\boxed{\text{SHIFT}}$ $\boxed{\text{CLEAR/} <}$

   Commodore — $\boxed{\text{SHIFT}}$ $\boxed{\text{CLR/HOME}}$

   TRS-80 — $\boxed{\text{CLEAR}}$

   Texas Instruments — CALL CLEAR

   Timex Sinclair — V (the CLS key)

5. It makes a space.

6. SYNTAX ERROR (or the abbreviation). (Exception: The TI says INCORRECT STATEMENT.)

7. O with a slash through it, or Ø (except on the Atari and TI).

2.
1, 2, 3 — Run!

To talk to your computer you must learn to speak its language. The language your computer uses is called BASIC. (If you like trivia, you may want to know that BASIC stands for Beginners' All-purpose Symbolic Instruction Code.)

1. Printing in BASIC.

One of the most important words in the BASIC language is PRINT. Let's see what happens when you tell the computer to PRINT some different things.

Type these commands into the computer, and see what the computer prints. (Ignore it if your computer prints READY or OK or some such message before the cursor. That just means it's ready for the next instruction.)

Note: Where you see RETURN, that means press the RETURN key. If you have a TRS-80, Texas Instruments, or Timex Sinclair computer, press ENTER where you see RETURN.

1. You type PRINT 82 RETURN   What does the computer print?
2. You type PRINT 8 + 2 RETURN   What does the computer print?
3. You type PRINT 8 − 2 RETURN   What does the computer print?
4. You type PRINT 8 * 2 RETURN   What does the computer print?
5. You type PRINT 8 / 2 RETURN   What does the computer print?

6. You type **PRINT HELLO** RETURN   What does the computer print?
7. You type **PRINT "HELLO"** RETURN   What does the computer print?
8. You type **PRINT "8 + 2"** RETURN   What does the computer print?

(If you typed everything correctly, the computer should have printed: **82**, **1Ø, 6, 16, 4, Ø, HELLO,** and **8 + 2**.)

Notice that the * symbol means "times" and the / sign means "divided by" to the computer. Do not try to type × for multiplication. The computer won't know what you mean.

When you tell the computer to print a math problem, it automatically prints the answer, unless you type the problem inside quotation marks.

Finally, notice that when you want the computer to print a word, you must put the word inside quotation marks.

It's very important when you type commands into the computer to do them in exactly the right way. Computers are pretty dumb about figuring out what you mean. If you haven't yet made a mistake in your typing, let's try it to see what the computer will do.

Suppose your finger slips and you type **PRIN 82**. If you remember Chapter 1, you may be able to predict what the computer will tell you when it doesn't understand you. Try it and see.

Did you get that error message again? Any time you see that, just look back over what you typed and see if you can find your mistake.

2. Your First Program.

Now — get ready. You are about to write a real computer program. *A program is a list of instructions to the computer.*

So far you have only told the computer to do one thing at a time, and it did that thing right away. When you write a program, you give the computer a whole list of instructions, but the computer waits to start doing those things. You must number your directions in the order you want the computer to do them. When you begin a line with a number, you tell the computer: "Wait to do this. Remember this direction, but don't do it until someone tells you to."

Before you start any program you should type the word **NEW**. This tells the computer you are beginning a new program.

Type this program exactly as it appears. Be sure you type the numbers!
Remember: On the TRS-80, TI, or Timex Sinclair you will use ENTER instead of RETURN .

```
NEW RETURN
1  PRINT "I" RETURN
2  PRINT "LOVE" RETURN
3  PRINT "YOU" RETURN
```

3. Run = Start the Program.

Right now the computer is remembering everything you typed into it. But it will not *do* any of those things until you tell it to. The BASIC word that tells the computer to start doing the program is **RUN**.

Type **RUN** RETURN and the computer should print:

```
I
LOVE
YOU
```

You can erase the screen, and the computer will still remember the program. Try it. Clear the screen. (If you've forgotten how, look back to Section 5 in Chapter 1. Or check Appendix I: Quick Reference Guide.) Then type **RUN** RETURN again.

Every time you type **RUN** the computer will keep on telling you that it loves you, because that's what you told it to remember.

4. Adding Lines to Your Program.

Let's add two more lines to this program. Type:

```
4  PRINT"DO YOU" RETURN
5  PRINT "LOVE ME?" RETURN
RUN RETURN
```

and the computer should print the whole program, starting with line 1, like this:

```
I
LOVE
YOU
DO YOU
LOVE ME?
```

5. Starting Over: Erase with NEW.

Remember, you cannot erase the program by erasing the screen. The program is still in the memory of the computer where you can't see it (the same way you can have a thought in your head without saying it out loud).

One way to erase the program is to turn off the computer. The other way is to type **NEW**. Typing **NEW** will erase the program you now have inside the computer and make the computer ready to start a new program.

Test this. First type RUN RETURN and you will see the familiar message: I LOVE YOU DO YOU LOVE ME? Then type NEW RETURN RUN RETURN. What happens? Nothing happens, because you have erased the program from the computer's memory. So be careful with that word **NEW**. Type it only when you are very sure you want to wipe out your program.

6. Mixing Up Numbers.

Let's see what happens when you mix up the order of your directions.
Note: From now on we will not tell you to type RETURN at the end of a line. You will have to remember to press the RETURN or ENTER key at the end of every line.

```
NEW
2 PRINT "MY"
1 PRINT "KISS"
4 PRINT "DOG"
```

```
3 PRINT "SMELLY"
RUN
```

What does the computer print? Notice that the computer printed the words in the order of the numbers, not in the order you typed them.

7. List = Print the Directions.

To see the way the computer stored or remembered the program, type LIST. The computer should print:

```
1 PRINT "KISS"
2 PRINT "MY"
3 PRINT "SMELLY"
4 PRINT "DOG"
```

LIST is another very important word in the BASIC language. To the computer, LIST means: "Show your program on the screen" or "Print the whole list of instructions for this program in order."

Remember that RUN will make the computer actually do the instructions in the program. LIST will make the computer show you what those instructions are. To make sure you understand the difference between these two words, type RUN [RETURN] and then LIST [RETURN] several times. Notice how the computer responds to each command.

If you want to list just part of the program, type LIST, followed by the line number(s) you want to see. For example, type

```
LIST 3 [RETURN]
```

and the computer should print

```
3 PRINT "SMELLY"
```

(The Timex Sinclair will print line 3, and every line after that.)

8. Making Changes.

If you decide to change part of your program, you don't have to start all over again. All you need to do is retype the line or lines you want to change. Suppose you decide you'd rather wash your dog than kiss him. Change line 1 by typing this:

```
1 PRINT "WASH"
RUN
```

and the computer should print

```
WASH
MY
SMELLY
DOG
```

When you list the program, you will see that the computer has erased your old line 1 from the program and put the new line in its place.

If you want to erase a whole line, just type the line number and RETURN (or ENTER). Our poor dog gets insulted when we call him smelly, so let's take that line out. Type

```
3 RETURN
RUN
```

and the computer should print

```
WASH
MY
DOG
```

And now when you type LIST, you should see

```
1 PRINT "WASH"
2 PRINT "MY"
4 PRINT "DOG"
```

9. Number by Tens.

Tip: Instead of numbering programs starting 1, 2, 3, 4, etc., programmers usually go by tens: 10, 20, 30, 40, etc. That makes it easy to go back and insert lines you might think of later.

Type this

```
NEW
10 PRINT "I AM"
```

        2Ø PRINT "A BOY"
        RUN

and the computer obediently prints

        I AM
        A BOY

Now let's add a new line to this program for the girls. Type

        15 PRINT "NOT"
        RUN

What does the computer print now? Type LIST, to see how the computer inserted your new line 15 in the right place:

        10 PRINT "I AM"
        15 PRINT "NOT"
        20 PRINT "A BOY"

10. Something Like a Post Office.

Think about writing in BASIC this way. When you press the keys, you are sending messages, or notes, to your computer. For example, if you type

        PRINT "LOLLIPOP"

as soon as you press RETURN or ENTER you are delivering the note to your computer. The computer reads the note, does what it says (if it can understand the message), and immediately forgets about it. *But* when you type

        1Ø PRINT "LOLLIPOP"

it is like putting your note into an envelope, which is labeled Number 10. Imagine that inside the computer are thousands of little envelopes, each with a different number on the outside. You could fill up each one of those numbered envelopes with a different message (or program line). The computer keeps your messages in those envelopes, just holding on to them, until you type:

        RUN

RUN means: "Open every envelope with a message, in order, and follow the directions inside." The notes will then stay in those envelopes until you tell the computer to get rid of them, usually by typing NEW. When you type:

        NEW

it is like telling the computer: "Throw away everything in all your envelopes, and get ready to insert some new messages." (Turning off the computer also empties out all the messages.)

11. When Your Computer Complains.

Sometimes you will accidentally put the wrong message in the computer's "envelopes." When that happens the computer will send you a complaint, or an error message. There are two ways you can fix your mistake. One way is like tearing up your letter and starting over. To do that with a computer message, just type the line number and the whole line over again, then press RETURN or ENTER .

The other way is like erasing only the wrong parts of the letter and correcting them. That involves using the editing functions on your computer. To find out more about those, turn to Appendix III.

Please remember, though, that the computer can only tell you when you have made a mistake in its language. Your computer speaks BASIC, not English. So if you type

> 1Ø PRIMT "HELLO"

you will get an error message. If you type

> 1Ø PRINT "HELO"

the computer assumes that HELO is a perfectly good English word and prints it just the way you typed it.

When you misspell a BASIC word on the Apple or Commodore, they will just tell you **SYNTAX ERROR IN 1Ø**, for example, and leave it up to you how to proceed from there. The TRS-80 and Atari go a little further. If you have one of those two computers, read this section to be sure you understand what to do when you get an error message.

TRS   On the TRS-80 (Model I or III) when you try to run a program with an error, the computer will automatically put you in Edit mode. Try this. Type this line with a misspelled word:

```
10 PRNT "HI"
RUN
```

and the screen will show

```
?SN ERROR IN 10 (or SYNTAX ERROR IN 10)
READY
10
```

Line 10 is now ready and waiting for you to edit it. If you want to use the Edit mode, read Appendix III. If you don't want to use the Edit mode (and for a simple mistake like this it's probably not worth it), just press ENTER. The computer will again show you the whole line with the mistake. Press ENTER again and retype the line correctly.

If you have an Atari, it will tell you that you've made a typing mistake as soon as you press RETURN. It will do that by reprinting the line with the word ERROR after the line number, and highlighting the mistake. You can get things back on track by retyping the line correctly. (See Appendix III for more details.)

12. Keeping Out of Trouble.

Some rules to remember when writing a BASIC program are:
* The first thing you type (after NEW) is a line number.
* The second thing you type in each line is a BASIC word or symbol.
* English words go inside quotes; BASIC words and symbols stay outside the quotes.
* Always press RETURN or ENTER before you type a line number.

Following these rules carefully will prevent most beginners' problems. But you will still have times when your program does something unexpected, or you can't get it to work the way it should. When this happens, turn to the back of the book and find Appendix II: Troubleshooting to see if those suggestions will help you locate the source of the trouble.

If you have trouble remembering something like how to clear the screen on your computer, check Appendix I: Quick Reference Guide.

Practice 2

In Chapter 2 you learned some important words. Some of these words are: program, BASIC, PRINT, NEW, RUN, LIST. Look back over the chapter and answer these questions.

1. What word do you always type in when you want to erase an old program and start a new one?
2. What key do you press to tell the computer you have finished typing something?
3. What word tells the computer to show you the instructions (the numbered lines) for the program it is currently working on?
4. What word tells the computer to start doing the instructions in the program?
5. What will the computer print if you type PRINT 5 + 5?
6. What will the computer print if you type PRINT 5 * 5?
7. What will the computer print if you type this program?

   ```
   3 PRINT "ME ON"
   1 PRINT "COMPUTERS"
   2 PRINT "TURN"
   RUN
   ```

8. What will the computer print when you run this program?

   ```
   NEW
   1Ø PRINT 2 * 1
   2Ø PRINT "GOOD"
   3Ø PRINT 8 / 4
   4Ø PRINT "B"
   5Ø PRINT 6 − 2
   6Ø PRINT "GOT"
   7Ø PRINT 5 + 5
   ```

   (Read the above message fast, and you'll know what we hope you think about the computer lessons.)

9. What is the name of the language you are learning for your computer?
10. What do we call a set of numbered instructions to the computer?
11. What will the computer print if you type PRIMT 42?

Answers to Practice 2

1. NEW
2. RETURN (or ENTER)
3. LIST
4. RUN
5. 1∅
6. 25
7. COMPUTERS
   TURN
   ME ON
8. 2
   GOOD
   2
   B
   4
   GOT
   1∅
9. BASIC
10. program
11. SYNTAX ERROR (or the equivalent on your computer).
    The TI will print INCORRECT STATEMENT.
    On the Timex Sinclair it is impossible to type PRIMT.

3.
Drive the Computer Loopy

1. A Nonstop Program.

Type this program:

```
NEW
1Ø PRINT "XXXXXX"
2Ø GOTO 1Ø
RUN
```

What happens? You should see the computer print an endless string of X's along the left side of the screen. (Or if you're feeling friendly toward your computer, you might want to think that it is sending you a string of kisses.)

2. How to Stop It.

When you get tired of looking at X's, do this:

  🍎   Hold down the CTRL key and press the letter C.

  TRS ⅄   Press the BREAK key.

  Ꮯ   Press the RUN/STOP key.

  TI   Press FCTN 4.

  T/S   (You don't have to stop the Timex Sinclair. It automatically stops itself as soon as the screen fills up.)

41

3. How It Works.

You have just programmed a *loop,* like this:

```
10   Print "XXXXXX"
20   GOTO 10
```

In line 10, you told the computer to print some X's. Then in line 20 you told it to go back to line 10 and do the same thing over again. When you run this program, the poor computer will just keep on going around in circles, from 10 to 20 to 10 to 20, etc., etc. It would print X's forever until you pulled the plug, or broke into the program (with **BREAK, CTRL C,** or **RUN/STOP,** etc.). Since this loop has no end, we call it an *infinite loop.*

GOTO is the word used in BASIC to make the computer skip around in a program. The word **GOTO** is always followed by a line number.

Practice. Change line 10 to make the computer print your name, or any other message you would like to see repeated over and over again.

4. A Larger Loop.

You can have as many program lines as you want included in your loop. For example:

```
NEW
10 PRINT "THIS PROGRAM"
20 PRINT "IS DRIVING"
30 PRINT "ME LOOPY!"
40 GOTO 10
RUN
```

A diagram of this program would look like this:

```
10
20
30
40
```

When the program runs off the top of the screen like that and keeps going, we say it is *scrolling.* There are certain things you can do on some computers to interrupt or slow down the scrolling without breaking off the program. Here's a list:

Hold down the CTRL key and type **S.** This will "freeze" the screen (stop the scrolling). When you press any key, the scrolling will begin where it left off.

ʎ Hold down the CTRL key and type 1 to interrupt the scrolling. Typing CTRL 1 again will restart it.

TRS Hold down the SHIFT key and press @. Hit any key to continue.

ᑲVIC There is no key on the Commodore to freeze the screen. However, on the VIC or 64 you can slow down the scrolling to make it easier to read by holding down the CTRL key. As soon as you let up the CTRL key it will speed up again.

ᑲPET On the PET you must press RUN/STOP . If you want to keep going from the point where you stopped, type CONT (for CONTinue). (This will also work on the VIC.)

TI The TI scrolls so slowly you don't need to freeze it.

T/S The Timex Sinclair does not scroll; it stops when the screen is full.

5. Using the semicolon(;).

The semicolon looks like a dot above a comma. You should find it on the right side of your keyboard (except on the Timex Sinclair, where it is over the X). A semicolon outside quotation marks tells the computer not to start a new line. Here's how it works:

```
NEW
10 PRINT "HE";
20 PRINT "ART"
RUN
```

Did you expect to see the computer print these two lines as one word? The semicolon made the computer print line 20 right after line 10, on the same line of the screen.

You can combine the semicolon with GOTO to make programs that fill up the screen. Type this:

```
NEW
10 PRINT "X";
20 GOTO 10
RUN
```

When you run this program, you'll see the whole screen covered with X's. The semicolon makes the computer print all the X's right next to each other.

You might want to experiment with some different keys on your computer to see what kinds of patterns you can make on the screen with programs like this. For example, change line 10 to:

        10 PRINT "XO";

or,

        10 PRINT "<*>";

Practice. Write a program using the semicolon to fill up the screen with your name.

6. Jumping Ahead.

So far we have used GOTO to make the computer go backward in a program. You can also use GOTO to make the computer go forward and skip over lines in a program.

Type in the program we did at the end of Chapter 2:

        NEW
        10 PRINT "I AM"
        20 PRINT "A BOY"

Remember how we added line 15 to change that program for girls? Type in that line 15. (If you've forgotten what it was, turn back to Chapter 2 and look.) Run the program. It should print:

        I AM
        NOT
        A BOY

Now add one more line:

        12 GOTO 20

Run the program again. It should print

        I AM
        A BOY

List the program. It should look like this:

```
10 PRINT "I AM"
12 GOTO 20
15 PRINT "NOT"
20 PRINT "A BOY"
```

Trace some imaginary arrows on that program to show how it skips over line 15.

Practice 3

1. Think up a good slogan for your school. Write a program that will make the computer print your slogan over and over again.
2. What will the computer print if you type in this program and run it? *Think* before you answer.

```
10 PRINT "THIN";
20 PRINT "KING"
```

3. Look at this program:

```
10 PRINT "SMART PEOPLE"
20 PRINT "NEVER"
30 PRINT "MAKE"
40 PRINT "MISTAKES"
```

If you run this program now it will print

```
SMART PEOPLE
NEVER
MAKE
MISTAKES
```

What line could you add to this program to make it print

```
SMART PEOPLE
MAKE
MISTAKES
```

(Hint: Look at the last program in Chapter 3.)

Answers to Practice 3

1. (This is a sample program. You will have your own slogan in line 10. Or maybe your slogan will take more than one line.)

```
1Ø PRINT "DON'T BE A FOOL — COME TO SCHOOL"
2Ø GOTO 1Ø
```

2. THINKING

3. You would add line 15 (or any other number between 10 and 20):

```
15 GOTO 3Ø
```

4.
Your Number, Please?

1. Changing Letters into Numbers.

In English we use letters to spell words and we use numbers for counting. But in BASIC letters and numbers are a little more mixed up. A letter can either be a part of a word, or it can be used to stand for a number. In fact, a letter in BASIC by itself *always* stands for some number. You tell the computer what number the letter equals, like this:

    H = 5 (or LET H = 5)
    PRINT H

and the computer prints 5 (if you remembered to hit the $\boxed{\text{RETURN}}$ or $\boxed{\text{ENTER}}$ key). Now try this:

    PRINT H + 3

Do you understand why the computer printed 8? Remember in Chapter 2 when you told the computer to print 8 + 2? It printed 10. This is another example of the same type of statement. Since you have told the computer that H equals 5, when the computer sees H + 3 it "thinks" 5 + 3. And any time you tell the computer to print a math problem, it gets right to work and prints the answer (unless, of course, the problem is inside quotation marks).

If you don't tell the computer what a letter equals, the computer assumes that it equals zero. Type

47

  PRINT A

and the computer prints Ø.

  Now type

  A = 7 (or LET A = 7)

  PRINT A

  You have changed A from a zero to a 7. You can change it again, if you want, into any number you choose. Remember, you're in charge here. Pick your favorite number and tell the computer that A equals that number.

Note: On most computers the use of the word LET in such statements is optional. The computer will do exactly the same thing whether you say H = 5 or LET H = 5. On the Timex Sinclair, however, you *must* use the LET statement.

2. Add Up Your Letters.

What happens now if you tell the computer to put H and A together? In English, if you saw H + A, you would probably think of the word "ha." But when the computer sees H + A, it thinks of a math problem. What number would H + A equal to the computer right now? Take a guess, then tell the computer to PRINT H + A and see if you were right.

  H and A (or any other letters you choose) are *variables.* The word "variable" means something that can change. You can tell the computer to change a letter into any number you want.

  Whatever the variable equals at any point is the *value* of the variable. When you tell the computer that H=5, we say you are assigning the value of 5 to the variable H. A variable is really only a label. You can hang that label on any number and switch the labels around any way you want and as often as you want.

  Remember in Chapter 2 we said that line numbers in your programs were like labels on envelopes. The instructions in each line were the messages you put in the envelopes. A variable name, like A, N, or Z, is the label for another kind of "envelope." The only things that will fit into these envelopes are numbers. The envelopes with numbers on the outside hold messages (the program) but the envelopes with letters on the outside hold numbers. So when the computer finds the label A in the program, it goes to the "envelope" marked A, either to put something in or take something out.

3. What Happens with Big Numbers?

Actually, a variable can only stand for any number that isn't too long. Try this:

    N = 12345678910
    PRINT N

and you get something like 1.23456789E+10. That means you have to move the decimal point over 10 spaces to the right. Some computers can't remember any number that has more than 7 digits. Others can handle 8 or 9. Experiment to see the longest number your computer can remember. (The Timex Sinclair computer, instead of printing 1.23456789E+10, will round off the number. So you'll get, for example, 1234566900.)

Another thing to remember about big numbers: Don't use commas when you type them. The number one hundred twenty-five thousand should be typed 125000. Try telling the computer that N=125,000 (with the comma) just to see the error message you get.

4. Now for a Program.

You can put variables in a program, like this:

    NEW   or, for the Timex Sinclair:
    10 N = 2   10 LET N=2
    20 X = 5   20 LET X=5
    30 PRINT N + X   30 PRINT N+X

What will that program print? Run it and see if you guessed correctly. Notice that lines 10 and 20 don't make anything happen on the screen when you run the program. They tell the program to do something *inside* the computer, but only the word PRINT makes a message appear on the screen.

Now change lines 10 and 20 to give the variables some different values.

5. Put in Some INPUT.

Variables are very useful in a program when combined with the BASIC word INPUT. The INPUT statement makes the computer stop the program until the person at the keyboard types something and hits RETURN or ENTER.

To see how INPUT works, type this one-line program:

```
NEW
1Ø INPUT N
RUN
```

and you should see a question mark appear, followed by the cursor. (On the Timex Sinclair, you will see only the cursor, with an L inside it.) That means the computer is waiting for you to tell it what N equals. It wants you to INPUT a number to stand for N. (Or, it wants you to PUT a number IN the N "envelope.") Type in any number, and press RETURN or ENTER. Then type PRINT N, and the computer should print the number you just typed in. By using INPUT you can make your programs do something different every time you run them.

The word INPUT in a program means "The computer needs some information here." But you must be sure that your program explains what kind of information it wants. So whenever you write an INPUT line, you should put a PRINT line before it. For example, you might begin this program by saying

```
5 PRINT "TYPE A NUMBER."
```

Now when you run the program it becomes clear what you want the person at the keyboard to type.

Note: On some computers (for example, the Apple and TRS-80) you don't have to put your PRINT statement in a separate line when you use INPUT. Instead of saying this:

```
5 PRINT "TYPE A NUMBER."
1Ø INPUT N
```

you can say

```
1Ø INPUT "TYPE A NUMBER"; N
```

But in our programs we will always do it the first way and keep PRINT and INPUT in separate lines.

Add one more line to that program:

    2Ø PRINT N; "IS A NICE NUMBER."

Now list and you should see:

    5 PRINT "TYPE A NUMBER."

    1Ø INPUT N

    2Ø PRINT N; "IS A NICE NUMBER."

Run the program several times. Put in a different number every time, and notice how the computer always inserts your number for the letter N in line 20. *Note:* The semicolon in line 20 above is optional on most computers. But on the TI or Timex Sinclair you must include it.

6. Numbers Only, Please.

What would happen if you typed a word instead of a number for your INPUT? Try it. Type RUN, and when you see the question mark or cursor, type your name instead of a number. What message do you get?

    That message means you gave the computer the wrong kind of information and it wants you to do it over. A word cannot be typed in for INPUT N. You must type in a number to stand for N. (We'll find out in the next chapter how to tell the computer to expect a word for INPUT.) Right now, to keep the computer happy, type in a number before you go on.

7. Program Some Problems.

Now let's make this program do something a little more fancy. Add these lines:

    3Ø PRINT "TYPE ANOTHER NUMBER."

    4Ø INPUT X

    5Ø PRINT "I CAN ADD THESE. THE TOTAL IS"

    6Ø PRINT N + X

    RUN

Here is a sample run of this program.

    TYPE A NUMBER

    ?6

```
6 IS A NICE NUMBER.
TYPE ANOTHER NUMBER
?5
I CAN ADD THESE. THE TOTAL IS
11
```

Now *you* run it several times, with different numbers each time.

You may pick any letter in the alphabet to stand for your variable numbers. The program would work exactly the same way if you used P and Q instead of X and N.

There are two important things to watch out for with variables:

1. Use a different letter for each different variable.

2. Always make sure the variables are *outside* the quotation marks.

Think about the "envelope idea" when you are using variables in different ways in your programs:

A = 5 means "Put the number 5 into the envelope marked A."

PRINT A means "Show me what's in the A envelope."

INPUT A means "Hold the A envelope open until someone puts a number in it."

8. A Program to Check Your Homework.

Suppose you had some addition problems for homework, and you wanted to check your answers. This program would do that even more easily than a calculator. Of course, you have to type RUN every time you put in a new problem. But you could add a line to the program to make it automatically start over again after each problem. If you think back to Chapter 3, you will remember how to do that. Just add this:

```
70 GOTO 50
```

Now the program will just keep going and let you keep typing in your problems until you stop it.

Note: To stop this program now you must break in as you did with the GOTO programs in Chapter 3. But on some computers you must push an extra key to break in when your program is stopped at an INPUT line, waiting for you to answer.

Here's how to break into your program when it's stopped at an INPUT line:

    🍎   Press CTRL C and RETURN .

    C=   PET only: Press RUN/STOP and RETURN .

    C=   VIC or 64: With your left hand hold down the RUN/STOP key while with your right hand you press the RESTORE key.

TRS ⅄   Press the BREAK key.

TI   Hold down the FCTN key and press 4.

T/S   Hold down SHIFT and press A. (This equals STOP.)

It would be easy to change this program to do other kinds of problems besides addition. For example, you could make it multiply the two numbers N and X together, instead of adding them. You would only have to change two lines. (Remember, the times sign on the computer is *, not ×. And if you want to divide, this sign / means "divided by.")

List the program, figure out which two lines you would change, and try it.

9. Saving and Loading.

If you want to save this program to use again, you should store it on the tapes or disks used by your computer. The command SAVE (or on some computers, CSAVE, for cassette tapes) tells the computer to put the program onto disk or tape, in the form of magnetically coded signals. When you want to use the program at some later time, you insert that tape or disk and type the command LOAD (or CLOAD) to send these coded signals back into the computer's memory. The specific steps to follow vary with each computer. If you don't know how to save a program, this would be a good time to learn. Get the instruction manual that comes with your computer and find the page that tells you how to save programs. Follow the directions, and when you've got the program saved, practice loading it in again.

10. A Word to the Wise . . .

About **INPUT**: Remember, **INPUT** puts a question mark on the screen and makes the computer stop and wait for you. When you see the question mark, followed by the cursor, the computer is waiting for **INPUT** in a program. It is *not* ready for you to type **RUN, LIST, NEW**, a program line, or any other **BASIC** commands. When you see the question mark, you must either answer the question or change the subject. And to change the subject, you must first **BREAK** out of the program, as described above. It's like being on the telephone — when you're in the middle of a call, you can't make another one until you first hang up the phone. Once you "call up" a program by typing **RUN**, you must either finish the program or "hang up" on it with **BREAK**, before you do anything else.

11. Feet into Inches.

You can use the computer to figure out all kinds of math problems. Sometimes the easiest way to do that is to use a formula in your program. For instance, since there are 12 inches in one foot, you could write a formula like this:

I = F * 12   or LET I = F * 12

I, of course, stands for the number of inches. Then you can use that formula in a program to change feet into inches:

```
NEW
10 PRINT "THIS PROGRAM WILL CHANGE FEET INTO INCHES."
20 PRINT "TYPE THE NUMBER OF FEET."
30 INPUT F
40 I = F * 12
50 PRINT F; "FEET = " ;I; " INCHES"
```

In line 40 you taught the computer the rule for changing feet to inches. That line makes the computer do the math "in its head." After line 40 the computer will remember what I equals and put in that number when you tell it to print I in line 50. (Remember, on the Timex Sinclair, line 40 must say LET I = F * 12.)

Look carefully at line 50. Notice how the quotation marks are put around the words and the equal sign, but the variables F and I are *outside* the quotes. Because the letters are outside the quotes the computer automatically recognizes them as variables and therefore prints the numbers that they stand for.

Run that program a few times putting in different numbers for INPUT.

12. A Weighty Program.

Changing feet into inches may occasionally be useful, but it's sort of boring. Let's write a program that will figure out something a little more interesting — the total weight (approximately) of everyone in your class.

Before you can write this program, you need to know the average weight of people at different ages. If you are in fifth grade, and you know that an average fifth-grader weighs 71 pounds, you can figure out approximately how much everyone in your whole class would weigh. Just multiply 71 pounds by the number of people in your class. So if you have 25 kids in your class, all together they would weigh 25 times 71 pounds, or 1775 pounds.

The formula you use is: total Weight (W) equals number of Kids (K) times average number of Pounds per kid (P).

You could write that:

$$W = K * P \qquad \text{or LET } W = K * P$$

Here are some average weights for people in different grades:

Grade 1, 44 pounds	Grade 4, 64 pounds	Grade 7, 90 pounds
Grade 2, 48 pounds	Grade 5, 71 pounds	Grade 8, 100 pounds
Grade 3, 55 pounds	Grade 6, 80 pounds	

Before you start to write a program, you must think about all the steps the computer has to go through. Let's write out these steps first in English, and then we can translate them into BASIC.

- First we'll tell the computer what number to put in for P, taking it off the chart above.
- Next we'll ask the person running the program a question: "How many kids are in your class?"
- Then the computer will have to wait for the person to type a number. K will stand for that number.

• Then teach the computer the rule for figuring out the total weight, so it can do the math. In other words, just type the formula into the program.

• Since the computer now knows what numbers to put in for K and P, it has already figured out what W equals. In the last line it will print W, or the total weight of the whole class.

You might want to try to write the program yourself before you look at our example.

If you are in fifth grade, your program might look something like this:

```
NEW
10 P = 71 (or 10 LET P = 71)
20 PRINT "HOW MANY KIDS ARE IN YOUR CLASS?"
30 INPUT K
40 W = K * P (or 40 LET W = K * P)
50 PRINT "ALL TOGETHER THEY WOULD WEIGH "; W; " POUNDS"
```

If you wanted to write that program for sixth grade you would only have to change one short line. Which line is it and how would you change it? (Check your answer in the Answer section for this chapter.)

Practice 4

1. Write a program that will add any three numbers together. In other words, the program will look something like the example of the addition program in Chapter 4, but the computer will have to ask the person to type in three different numbers. So the program will have three INPUT lines and three different variables.

2. Write a program to make the computer figure out about how many hours you sleep in one year. Here are the steps the program must go through:

• First the computer will have to find out how many hours you sleep every night. (That will take a PRINT line for the question and an INPUT line for the answer — using H to stand for the number.)

- Then you tell the computer the formula it will need to figure out the answer. The total number of hours slept (S) equals the hours slept per night (H) times the number of days in a year (365). So the formula is S = H * 365.
- Finally the computer prints the total number of hours slept per year (S).

   When you have translated this into BASIC, your finished program should look something like the example in Section 11 of Chapter 4 (Feet into Inches).

3. Add some lines to the program in Problem 2 to make the computer figure out how many days old you were on your last birthday. To make it simple, we won't count leap years, so the formula would be D (for total number of days) = Y (number of years old) * 365.

   First, you will need to think about the steps involved, as we did in Problem 2. Then put those steps into your BASIC program.

4. Add to the program in Problems 2 and 3, to tell you how many hours you have slept in your whole life. The formula would be T (total hours slept) = S * Y.

5. Write a program to compute a baseball player's batting average. The formula is:

   Take the number of times at bat (B).

   Subtract the number of walks (W).

   Divide that answer (B−W) into the number of hits (H) to get the average (A). The formula looks like this:

   A = H / (B − W).

   The times at bat, hits, and walks should be INPUT lines in your program.

Answers to Practice 4

Answer to question in Section 12:

   You would change line 10. For sixth grade, line 10 should say P = 8∅ (or LET P = 8∅). For a fourth-grader it would be P = 64.

Note: In all answers, the letters you choose for the variables and the wording in your **PRINT** statements may be slightly different from ours. These are only sample programs.

1. 10 PRINT "TYPE A NUMBER."
    20 INPUT A
    30 PRINT "TYPE ANOTHER NUMBER."
    40 INPUT B
    50 PRINT "TYPE ONE MORE NUMBER."
    60 INPUT C
    70 PRINT "THE SUM OF THOSE NUMBERS IS "; A + B + C

2. 10 PRINT "HOW MANY HOURS DO YOU SLEEP EVERY NIGHT?"
    20 INPUT H
    30 S = H * 365
    40 PRINT "YOU SLEEP ";S; " HOURS A YEAR."

3. 50 PRINT "HOW MANY YEARS OLD ARE YOU?"
    60 INPUT Y
    70 D = Y * 365
    80 PRINT "YOU WERE ";D;" DAYS OLD ON YOUR BIRTHDAY."

4. 90 T = S * Y
    100 PRINT "YOU HAVE SLEPT ";T;" HOURS IN YOUR LIFE."

5. 10 PRINT "TYPE THE NUMBER OF TIMES AT BAT."
    20 INPUT B
    30 PRINT "NUMBER OF WALKS"
    40 INPUT W
    50 PRINT "NUMBER OF HITS"
    60 INPUT H
    70 A = H / (B − W)
    80 PRINT "THE BATTING AVERAGE IS ";A

A sample run of that program might look like this:

    TYPE THE NUMBER OF TIMES AT BAT.
    ? 30

NUMBER OF WALKS
? *4*
NUMBER OF HITS
? *8*
THE BATTING AVERAGE IS .3Ø7692308

Of course, we don't usually see batting averages that look like that number. Just drop off everything after the first three numbers to make the batting average .307. (Actually, if you know about rounding off, you'll realize it should be .308.)

5.
All Tied Up in Strings

In Chapter 4 you learned how to write programs where the variables were numbers. You will probably have even more fun writing programs where the variables can be words. These programs will let the computer seem to carry on a real conversation with you.

1. Let's Experiment.

When your variable was a number, you typed something like this:

A=6 (or LET A=6)

Remember: You must use **LET** on the Timex Sinclair. On others, it's optional.

What happens if you try to make your variable A stand for a word? Let's see. Type this:

A= HELLO (or LET A=HELLO)
PRINT A

and your computer prints a zero. This may remind you of something in Chapter 2. Remember, to make the computer print a word, you had to type **PRINT "HELLO"**. When you didn't use the quotes, the computer gave you a zero.

Well, those quotation marks worked before. Maybe they will again. Try this:

A="HELLO"

No, that didn't work either. What did the computer tell you this time?

That error message means you tried to put in a word where the computer wanted a number. In BASIC a plain letter (or group of letters) can only be used to stand for a number.

To tell the computer to expect a *word* for a variable, you use a letter (any letter in the alphabet), plus a dollar sign ($). For example — **A$**.

The computer word for this **$** symbol is *string*. So when you see **A$** in a program, you say "A-string." Actually, a string can be any combination of letters, numbers, or graphics symbols.

A$,B$,C$, etc., are examples of labels for a third type of "envelope" in the computer's memory. Remember, the "envelopes" labeled with numbers contain program lines. The "envelopes" labeled with plain letters contain numbers. And the "envelopes" labeled with a letter plus a dollar sign may contain anything you can type on the keyboard.

2. Strings and Spaces.

Here's how it works. (But if you have an Atari read the special note just below first.)

```
        A$="HELLO" (or LET A$="HELLO")
        PRINT A$
```

Special note for the Atari computer only: Whenever you use a string variable on an Atari, you must first tell the computer how long the word might be. So on the Atari you should type this:

```
  ⅄     DIM A$ (1Ø)
        A$="HELLO"
        PRINT A$
```

The **DIM** line tells the computer that whatever word or words you type in for **A$** will have no more than 10 letters or spaces. (**DIM** stands for **DIM**ension, which is another word for size.) If you forget to type in the **DIM** line, the computer will send you an error message. It's okay to make the **DIM** number longer than the word you put in for **A$**, but it can't be shorter. (In other words if you say **DIM A$(1Ø)**, you can make **A$=**"HELLO", because **HELLO** has less than 10 letters. You can't make **A$=**"HELLO THERE" because that adds up to 11 letters and spaces.) The biggest your **DIM** number can be is 255.

Now, if you spelled everything right and remembered your quotation marks, you've finally made the computer print **HELLO**.

Try this:

>   B$="SAM" (or LET B$="SAM")
>   PRINT A$;B$

⅄   Remember for the Atari you must first type

>   DIM B$(1Ø)

Did your computer print **HELLOSAM**—all one word? Here's one way you can make it space:

>   PRINT A$,B$

The comma tells the computer to space over and start a new column. (The number of spaces in the column and the number of columns on one line depend on what kind of computer you have.)

If you just want to leave one space between words, you must put your space inside the quotation marks, like this:

>   B$= " SAM"

Now type

>   PRINT A$;B$

Practice this. Try making **B$** equal your name (unless your name is Sam, of course, and you've already done it). Then make the computer say hello to you. Next use some other letters to create new string variables. Tell the computer to print your variables with commas between them, like this:

>   PRINT A$,B$,C$,D$

That way you'll find out where the columns start on your computer.

3. Introduce Yourself to Your Computer.

Now let's put string variables into programs with **INPUT** lines. Here is a sample program:

```
NEW
10 PRINT "WHAT IS YOUR NAME?"
20 INPUT N$
30 PRINT "NICE TO MEET YOU,";N$
RUN
```

ᛨ   On the Atari you must begin your program with a **DIM** statement in line 1, like this: 1 DIM N$(20)

Notice (in line 30) that **N$** must be outside the quotation marks. Variables can never be put inside quotation marks.

Run this program several times. Give the computer some different answers when it asks you "What is your name?"

4. A Colorful Example.

Here's another program using a string variable:

```
NEW
10 PRINT "WHAT IS YOUR FAVORITE COLOR?"
20 INPUT C$
30 PRINT "ONLY THE SMARTEST PEOPLE LIKE ";C$
```

ᛨ   Atari only, add this line: 1 DIM C$(20)

Run this program several times. Try giving the computer a silly answer when it asks for your favorite color. You'll find out that the computer doesn't know whether you actually typed in a color for an input. No one has taught the computer what is or is not a color, so it will keep right on with the program even if you tell it that your favorite color is spaghetti.

5. Triple Strings.

You can put lots of string variables in one program. Here's an example:

```
NEW
10 PRINT "WHAT IS YOUR NAME?"
20 INPUT N$
```

```
3Ø PRINT "WHO IS YOUR TEACHER?"
4Ø INPUT T$
5Ø PRINT "WHAT IS YOUR FAVORITE SUBJECT?"
6Ø INPUT S$
7Ø PRINT T$; " SAYS THAT ";N$; " IS VERY GOOD AT ";S$
```

On the Atari, add this line: 1 DIM N$(25),T$(25),S$(25)

Here is a sample run of this program. It will look different when you run it, of course.

```
WHAT IS YOUR NAME?
? TERRY
WHO IS YOUR TEACHER?
? MR. CHIPS
WHAT IS YOUR FAVORITE SUBJECT?
? RECESS
MR. CHIPS SAYS THAT TERRY IS VERY GOOD AT RECESS.
```

Note: In line 70 if you remember to type a space before and after the quotation marks, the computer will not run your words together.

6. Try It Yourself.

See if you can write a program like this:

First, the computer asks you what school you go to. (This will be a PRINT line.)

Second, it waits for your answer, and gives it a string variable code name. (This will be an INPUT line.)

Third, the computer prints _____ is the best! (In the blank the computer would print the name of your school when you run the program. In other words, the blank is the string variable.)

The last line of the program would make the computer print over and over again that your school is the best. (This will be a GOTO line, going back to the PRINT line just before.)

After you've written your own program, check it against our example:

```
NEW
10 INPUT "WHAT SCHOOL DO YOU GO TO?"
20 INPUT S$
30 PRINT S$; " IS THE BEST!";
40 GOTO 30
```
Ʌ   Atari, add: 1 DIM S$(25)

Note: The semicolon at the end of line 30 is optional.

Practice 5

1. Write a program with two string variables that would make the computer print something like this:

    PLEASE TYPE YOUR NAME
    ? *JENNY*
    NAME ONE PART OF YOUR BODY
    ? *NOSE*
    JENNY HAS A BEAUTIFUL NOSE.

(The words JENNY and NOSE would be typed in by the person running the program. So if John ran the program, he could type in JOHN and BIG TOE, and the computer would tell him, "JOHN HAS A BEAUTIFUL BIG TOE.")

Here are the steps the program must go through:

First, the computer asks you to type your name.

Second, it waits for your answer, and gives your answer a string variable code.

Third, it asks you to name one part of your body.

Fourth, it waits for that answer and gives it a code.

Fifth, it uses those answers to print "_____ (your name) has a beautiful _____ (part of your body)."

2. Think up your own programs using INPUT variables to make the computer print different things. For example, think of something silly you can have the computer tell your friends. Then write the program so different people can use it.

Answers to Practice 5

1.   10 PRINT "PLEASE TYPE YOUR NAME."
         20 INPUT N$
         30 PRINT "NAME ONE PART OF YOUR BODY."
         40 INPUT B$
         50 PRINT N$; " HAS A BEAUTIFUL ";B$

     λ   On the Atari, add: 1 DIM N$(25), B$(20)

2. Any program that works is right. Just be careful where you put your quotation marks!

6.
Just Fooling Around

In this chapter we'll be using the BASIC words you've learned so far to write some programs just for fun. But first, let's stop and review all the things you *have* learned.

1. Your BASIC Vocabulary.

You've learned two main types of words to use when you talk to the computer. *First* are the key words you actually put into your programs. These are words like PRINT, GOTO, and INPUT. You use those words in your numbered program lines to give the computer its instructions. Usually you want the computer to wait to do these things until you run the program. (This is called *deferred* execution.) The *second* type of BASIC words are the commands you use to talk directly to the computer — not inside a program. These are words like LIST, RUN, and NEW. Usually you want the computer to do these things right away. (This is called *immediate* or *direct* execution.)

Some other important things you've learned are:

1. How to use PRINT to make the computer do math problems or print words.

2. How to use variables like A or A$ in your programs.

3. How to use the comma and the semicolon to change the spacing in your programs.
4. How to stop a program in the middle.
5. How to erase a line from a program, and how to insert new lines into a program.
6. How to clear the screen, and how that is different from erasing the program.

If you're confused about any of these things, now is the time to stop and review them before you go on. (Check the index to help you find the right page.) In the rest of this chapter, you'll get some more practice using these various parts of BASIC to write some programs you can try out on your friends for fun.

2. Keep It Clean.

You'll notice that the last item on the list just above mentions clearing the screen. It's always a good idea when you start a program to do it on a nice clean screen. Instead of having to type the command that clears the screen every time you run a program, you can write a line into your program to make the computer erase the screen automatically. Doing this inside a program is a little different from doing it in immediate mode. Here's how you write that line in a program for each of our six computers:

  For the Apple, you type the line number and the word HOME, like this:
  10 HOME

  For the Atari, you type
  10 GRAPHICS 0
  or you may abbreviate this to
  10 GR.0
  (You may also type 10 PRINT "[ESC] [CTRL] [CLEAR]"
  or 10 PRINT "[ESC] [SHIFT] [CLEAR]"
  but GR.0 is much easier.)

  On the Commodore, you type the line number, PRINT, quotation mark, and hold down the [SHIFT] key while you type the [CLR/HOME] key, and another quotation mark, like this:

10 PRINT "[SHIFT] [CLR/HOME]"

When this appears on the TV screen, what you see is a little heart like this:

10 PRINT "♥"

TRS   On the TRS-80 you simply type the line number and CLS (which stands for Clear Screen), like this:

10 CLS

TI   On the TI you type, for example:

10 CALL CLEAR

T/S   On the Timex Sinclair you type the line number and press **V**, which appears as, for instance:

10 CLS

From now on when you see a line in a program that tells you to clear the screen, you'll have to remember the correct way to do it on your computer. We'll write it like this:

10 (clear the screen)

But you'll know that the words "clear the screen" won't mean anything to your computer. You'll have to translate them into your computer's language. If you forget, just look back to the above list, or check the quick reference list at the end of the book.

Here's an example of a program that uses that line twice:

NEW
10 (clear the screen)
20 PRINT "WHAT'S YOUR NAME?"
30 INPUT N$
40 (clear the screen)
50 PRINT "HI ";N$;
60 GOTO 50

⅄   On the Atari you add: 1 DIM N$(20)

This is one of those nonstop programs that you have to break into in order to make it end.

3. A Spacy Remark.

In that last program did it bother you to have your name run together with hi? If so, why don't you fix it by changing the last semicolon to a comma so line 50 looks like this:

```
5Ø PRINT "HI ";N$,
```

Remember, the comma makes the computer space over to another column. But if you're like most people, that's the kind of thing you tend to forget because you don't use it very much. One thing you can do to help you remember what the different parts of your program are doing is to put in remarks to yourself. Here's how that program might look with a REMark line:

```
1Ø (clear the screen)
2Ø PRINT "WHAT'S YOUR NAME?"
3Ø INPUT N$
4Ø (clear the screen)
45 REM COMMA MAKES COMPUTER SPACE IN COLUMNS
5Ø PRINT "HI ";N$,
6Ø GOTO 5Ø
```

The REMark in line 45 doesn't make the computer do anything. It just helps the person writing the program remember why he or she put something in there. When you write longer programs, sometimes you want to put in REM lines to keep you from getting confused. REM lines make it easier for a person to read your program listing and figure out why the program works a certain way.

4. A Crazy Letter.

Did you ever get one of those computerized letters that prints your name to make it look personal? You know the company is sending the same letter to thousands of people, but the computer makes it seem as though the letter is just for you. For example, Betty from Boston might get a letter like this:

```
DEAR BETTY,
    I HAVE JUST LEARNED THAT A GIANT GREEN POLAR BEAR WILL SOON
```

ATTACK BOSTON. IF YOU SEND ME 300 DOLLARS I WILL TELL YOU HOW TO KEEP THIS POLAR BEAR FROM BITING OFF YOUR NOSE.

On the other hand, Danny from Dallas might get a letter like this:

DEAR DANNY,

I HAVE JUST LEARNED THAT A GIANT PURPLE SHEEPDOG WILL SOON ATTACK DALLAS. IF YOU SEND ME 78 DOLLARS I WILL TELL YOU HOW TO KEEP THIS SHEEPDOG FROM BITING OFF YOUR BIG TOE.

As you can see, these letters are pretty much the same except for six things:

1. The name of the person
2. The city
3. The kind of animal
4. The color
5. The number of dollars
6. The part of the body

Imagine that you had written the letter with blanks where you would fill in those six things. (For example, the letter would start out "Dear _____, I have just learned that a giant _____ will soon attack _____.") Every blank is something that changes in each different letter. Before you can finish each letter, you have to fill in the blanks.

To the computer, each blank would be a *variable*. So when you write a computer program to print this letter, you have to start out by filling in the blanks — that is, by telling the computer what to put in for each variable. We'll do this with INPUT lines, like this:

```
NEW
5 (clear the screen)
1Ø PRINT "PLEASE TYPE YOUR NAME."
2Ø INPUT N$
3Ø PRINT "WHAT TOWN DO YOU LIVE IN?"
4Ø INPUT T$
5Ø PRINT "NAME A COLOR."
6Ø INPUT C$
7Ø PRINT "NAME AN ANIMAL."
```

```
80 INPUT A$
90 PRINT "TYPE A NUMBER."
100 INPUT N
110 PRINT "NAME A PART OF YOUR BODY."
120 INPUT B$
```

Ʌ   Remember, on the Atari add this line:

```
1 DIM N$(20),T$(20),C$(20),A$(20),B$(20)
```

Now — when we run the program, we will be filling in all those blanks. The last part of the program will be printing the letter. Let's put in a REM line to remind us that's what comes next.

```
130 REM START TO PRINT LETTER
135 (clear the screen)
140 PRINT "DEAR ";N$;","
150 PRINT "I HAVE JUST LEARNED THAT A GIANT ";C$
160 PRINT A$; " WILL SOON ATTACK " ;T$;"."
170 PRINT "IF YOU SEND ME ";N;" DOLLARS IMMEDIATELY,"
180 PRINT "I WILL TELL YOU HOW TO KEEP THIS ";A$;" FROM BITING
OFF YOUR ";B$;"."
```

Special note for TRS-80: The TRS-80 computer normally gives you enough space to store a total of 50 characters in all the string variables in your program. This program has 5 string variables. If you type in 4 names with 10 characters, you've used 40 characters. If you then try to make your fifth variable a word (or words) with 11 characters you'll be up to 51 and OUT OF STRING SPACE. So you'll get an error message. If that happens, type this: CLEAR 100. That will give you 100 letters and spaces worth of string space. You can write that line into your program if you wish, by typing:

```
1 CLEAR 100.
```

5. Changing the Letter.

After you run that a few times, you might start getting tired of that same letter. Let's take the same information, and use it to print a different letter. Here's one idea for another crazy letter:

DEAR (name),
I WAS SORRY TO HEAR YOUR (body part) TURNED (color) AND FELL OFF. I
HAVE A (animal) WITH AN EXTRA (body part) THAT I WILL SEND TO YOU
IN (city) FOR ONLY (number) DOLLARS.

You can easily change that program by putting in a GOTO line that will
make it skip over the first letter. Then start your new letter at line 190. Since
the first line (Dear _____) of both letters is the same, put your GOTO line
between 140 and 150, like this:

```
145 GOTO 19Ø
```

Before you look at the answer, try to write the new letter yourself. Begin at
line 190, using the variables we already have in the program to fill in the
blanks. Study lines 150 to 180 above to get the idea. After you've tried it, check
yourself against our example. (The answer is in the Answer section for Chapter
6.)

You might want to save this program on tape or disk, so you can change it
again to write your own crazy letter, either using the same variables, or some
different ones. If you do come back to this program again, you'll probably be
glad to have the REM lines to remind you what the program is doing and where
the letter starts.

6. String Together a Limerick.

Here's one more example of a program using string variables, this time to print
a limerick.

```
NEW
1Ø REM PROGRAM TO PRINT A LIMERICK
2Ø (clear the screen)
3Ø PRINT "PLEASE TYPE YOUR NAME."
4Ø INPUT N$
5Ø PRINT "NAME A PART OF YOUR BODY."
6Ø INPUT B$
7Ø PRINT "NAME AN OBJECT THAT RHYMES WITH ";B$;"."
8Ø INPUT F$
```

9Ø PRINT "NAME A PLACE (REAL OR IMAGINARY) THAT RHYMES WITH ";B$;"."

1ØØ INPUT P$

11Ø PRINT "TYPE A NUMBER."

12Ø INPUT N

13Ø (clear the screen)

14Ø PRINT N$; " 'S LIMERICK:"

15Ø PRINT "A PERSON NAMED ";N$;" FROM ";P$

16Ø PRINT "ONCE ATE ";N;" SERVINGS OF ";F$

17Ø PRINT "IT WAS QUITE A DISH"

18Ø PRINT "AND IT TASTED DELISH"

19Ø PRINT "BUT IT GAVE ";N$;" A VERY FAT ";B$;"."

Note: On the Atari add line 1:

⅄   1 DIM N$(25),B$(25),F$(25),P$(25)

Here's a sample run of that program:

PLEASE TYPE YOUR NAME.

? *PETER*

NAME A PART OF YOUR BODY.

? *LEG*

NAME AN OBJECT THAT RHYMES WITH LEG.

? *EGG*

NAME A PLACE (REAL OR IMAGINARY) THAT RHYMES WITH LEG.

? *DREGG*

TYPE A NUMBER.

? *29*

PETER'S LIMERICK:

A PERSON NAMED PETER FROM DREGG

ONCE ATE 29 SERVINGS OF EGG

IT WAS QUITE A DISH

AND IT TASTED DELISH

BUT IT GAVE PETER A VERY FAT LEG.

74

You might like to try making up your own program to write a limerick or some other type of poem.

Practice 6

1. Translate each of these English lines into a line in a BASIC program. The finished program will print a silly story. (Boy, girl, and food are variables.)

   10 The computer clears the screen.

   20 The computer asks you for the name of a boy in your class. (A PRINT line.)

   30 The computer waits for your answer, and gives your answer a string variable code name. (An INPUT line.)

   40 The computer asks you for the name of a girl in your class.

   50 The computer waits for your answer and gives it a code.

   60 The computer asks you to name a kind of food.

   70 The computer waits and codes.

   80 The computer clears the screen.

   90 Make a note to yourself to remind you that the story begins here.

   100 The computer prints (boy) loves (girl) and (girl) loves (boy).

   110 The computer prints (boy) brought (girl) some (food).

   120 The computer prints (boy) loves (food) but (girl) hates (food).

   130 The computer prints (girl) throws (food) at (boy).

   140 The computer prints And now (boy) hates (girl) and (girl) hates (boy).

2. Look back to the program in Section 4 of Chapter 6 (A Crazy Letter). In that program why does line 20 say INPUT N$ while line 100 says INPUT N?

3. Write a program using INPUT variables to make the computer print a fortune like this:

   IN (number) YEARS YOU WILL GO BY (a kind of travel) TO (a faraway place). YOU WILL MARRY SOMEONE WHO LOOKS LIKE (a TV star). YOU WILL HAVE (number) CHILDREN WHO WILL ALL LOOK LIKE (a movie monster.)

   Everything in the parentheses will be a variable in the program.

4. Make up your own program using INPUT variables to write a story.

Answers to Practice 6

Answer to the program in Section 5 (Changing the Letter): You should add new lines beginning after 180. Depending on how you divide up your letter, you may have more or fewer total lines in the program. The finished program should look something like this:

```
5 (clear the screen)
10 PRINT "PLEASE TYPE YOUR NAME."
20 INPUT N$
30 PRINT "WHAT TOWN DO YOU LIVE IN?"
40 INPUT T$
50 PRINT "NAME A COLOR."
60 INPUT C$
70 PRINT "NAME AN ANIMAL."
80 INPUT A$
90 PRINT "TYPE A NUMBER."
100 INPUT N
110 PRINT "NAME A PART OF YOUR BODY."
120 INPUT B$
130 REM START TO PRINT LETTER
135 (clear the screen)
140 PRINT "DEAR ";N$
145 GOTO 190
150 PRINT "I HAVE JUST LEARNED THAT A GIANT ";C$
160 PRINT A$; "WILL SOON ATTACK ";T$;"."
170 PRINT "IF YOU SEND ME ";N;" DOLLARS IMMEDIATELY,"
180 PRINT "I WILL TELL YOU HOW TO KEEP THIS ";A$;" FROM BITING
OFF YOUR ";B$;"."
185 REM END OF FIRST LETTER
190 PRINT "I WAS SORRY TO HEAR YOUR ";B$
200 PRINT "TURNED ";C$;" AND FELL OFF."
210 PRINT "I HAVE A ";A$;" WITH AN EXTRA ";B$
```

220 PRINT "THAT I WILL SEND TO YOU IN ";T$;" FOR ONLY ";N;" DOL-
LARS."

⋏   Atari: As noted earlier, do not forget the **DIM** line.

Note: The **REM** line at 185 is optional, but it will help you remember how the
program works. You may have your **PRINT** lines from 190 on beginning and
ending at different places in the letter. Any way you divide them up is okay —
but you can't make them too long, or your computer will complain.

Answers to Practice programs:

1.   1Ø (clear the screen — Use the correct line for your computer, as explained
in Section 2 of Chapter 6.)

2Ø PRINT "NAME A BOY IN YOUR CLASS."

3Ø INPUT B$

4Ø PRINT "NAME A GIRL IN YOUR CLASS."

5Ø INPUT G$

6Ø PRINT "NAME A FOOD."

7Ø INPUT F$

8Ø (clear the screen)

9Ø REM STORY BEGINS HERE

1ØØ PRINT B$;" LOVES ";G$;" AND ";G$;" LOVES ";B$;"."

11Ø PRINT B$;" BROUGHT ";G$;" SOME ";F$;"."

12Ø PRINT B$;" LOVES ";F$;" BUT ";G$;" HATES ";F$;"."

13Ø PRINT G$;" THROWS ";F$;" AT ";B$;"."

14Ø PRINT "AND NOW ";B$;" HATES ";G$;" AND ";G$;" HATES ";B$;"."

⋏   Atari, add: 1 DIM B$(2Ø),G$(2Ø),F$(2Ø)

2. Line 20 says **N$** because you are supposed to type a word, and you must use
a string variable to stand for a word. Line 40 says **N** because you are supposed to type a number, and you should use a plain letter to stand for a
number. (Actually you could use a string variable to stand for the number,
as long as you weren't planning to do any math with the number. But it's a
good idea to stay in the habit of using string variables for words and nu-
meric variables for numbers.)

3.   1Ø (clear the screen)

```
2Ø PRINT "TYPE A NUMBER."
3Ø INPUT N
4Ø PRINT "TYPE A KIND OF TRAVEL."
5Ø INPUT T$
6Ø PRINT "NAME A FARAWAY PLACE."
7Ø INPUT P$
8Ø PRINT "NAME A TV STAR."
9Ø INPUT S$
1ØØ PRINT "TYPE A NUMBER."
11Ø INPUT X
12Ø PRINT "NAME A MOVIE MONSTER."
13Ø INPUT M$
14Ø (clear the screen)
15Ø REM FORTUNE BEGINS HERE
16Ø PRINT "IN ";N;" YEARS YOU WILL GO BY ";T$
17Ø PRINT "TO ";P$;"."
18Ø PRINT "YOU WILL MARRY SOMEONE WHO LOOKS LIKE ";S$;"."
19Ø PRINT "YOU WILL HAVE ";X;" CHILDREN WHO WILL ALL LOOK
LIKE ";M$;"."
```

ꓕ   Atari, add: 1 DIM T$(25),P$(25),S$(25),M$(25)

4. Any program that works is right.

7.
Yes and No with IF and THEN

In many programs you want the computer to react differently according to what **INPUT** it gets. For example, your program might ask a question that could be answered "yes" or "no." You would want the computer to say one thing in answer to "yes" and another thing in answer to "no." In these cases, you use the BASIC words **IF** and **THEN**.

1. Your Computer Answers Back.

Type this sample program.
Note: If you have a Texas Instruments or Timex Sinclair computer, go to the end of this chapter for special instructions.

```
NEW
10 PRINT "DO YOU LIKE ME?"
20 INPUT A$
30 IF A$="YES" THEN PRINT "I LIKE YOU TOO."
40 IF A$="NO" THEN PRINT "YOU ARE A SNOB."
```
人   Atari, add: 1 DIM A$(10)

Warning: Be careful not to type any extra spaces inside the quotes in lines 30 and 40. Typing " YES", for example, would confuse the computer into thinking your answer had to be "yes" with a space in front of it.

Run this program, first answering "yes" to the computer's question, and then answering "no."

Do you understand how lines 30 and 40 work? In line 20 you told the computer that **A\$** would stand for whatever answer you (or whoever runs the program) type(s) in. In line 30 the computer checks to see if this answer (**A\$**) is yes. **IF** the answer is "yes," **THEN** the computer prints "I like you, too." **IF** the answer is "no" (line 40), **THEN** the computer comes back with "You are a snob." **IF** and **THEN** allow your programs to make choices.

Now see what happens if you answer anything other than "yes" or "no." For example, answer "maybe." What happens? Nothing happens, of course, because you haven't told the computer what to say in that case. In fact, you could even type an answer like "Nope," and the computer would not have any idea that "nope" means the same as "no."

What you need to do is to add one more line that will tell the computer what to do if a person gives any other answer besides "yes" or "no." We'll just have the computer politely ask you to answer "yes" or "no." Then we'll make it go back to ask the question ("Do you like me?") again.

In order to do this, you will have to have two BASIC statements in line 50, **PRINT** and **GOTO**. Whenever you combine two statements like that in one line, you must put a punctuation mark between them. The punctuation you use to separate two statements is a colon, which looks like two dots, one on top of the other(:). Here's our new line:

```
50 PRINT "PLEASE TYPE YES OR NO.":GOTO 10
```

Add that line, then run the program. You will see that the program now works fine if you answer "Maybe" or "I don't know" or anything *except* yes or no. But it doesn't work so well when you *do* answer yes or no.

2. The Bug Meets Its End.

By adding line 50 we have created a *bug* (that is, a problem) in the program. The bug is that the program does not stop when it ought to. Now we have to *debug,* or fix, our mistake so the program works the way we want it to.

Fortunately, this bug is a very easy one to fix. What do you want the program to do when someone answers "yes" or "no"? You want it to stop right there, don't you? So let's just tell the computer to end the program as soon as it gets an answer of either "yes" or "no."

First, break into the program by hitting the key (or keys) to stop the program when it is stalled at an input line. If you've forgotten what to press, go back and check Chapter 4. (Or use the Quick Reference Guide, Appendix I.) Now all you have to do is to add the word END at the end of line 30 and line 40. END simply means "This is the end of this program." Don't forget, you'll have to put in a colon first, because you'll be putting two statements in one line.

Here's how the finished program should look:

```
10 PRINT "DO YOU LIKE ME?"
20 INPUT A$
30 IF A$="YES" THEN PRINT "I LIKE YOU TOO.":END
40 IF A$="NO" THEN PRINT "YOU ARE A SNOB.":END
50 PRINT "PLEASE TYPE YES OR NO.":GOTO 10
```

Now the computer will know to end the program as soon as it gets a "yes" or "no" answer. The only way it gets to line 50 is when the person does not type in "yes" or "no."

3. Teach Your Computer Right from Wrong.

Sometimes you want to make up quiz programs in which the computer tells you if your answer is right or wrong. A symbol you will need for this is <> (or ><). This symbol is made up of the signs for "less than" and "greater than" put together, and it means the same as "not equal to." Here's a program using this symbol.

```
NEW
10 PRINT "HOW MANY 3 CENT STAMPS IN A DOZEN?"
20 INPUT A
30 IF A=12 THEN PRINT "CORRECT"
40 IF A<>12 THEN PRINT "FOOLED YOU!"
50 PRINT "THERE ARE ALWAYS 12 IN A DOZEN."
```

Line 40 means "If you type in any number that is not 12, the computer will tell you it fooled you."

Try that program on grownups. It seems to fool them more often than kids. They are usually more likely to say that the answer should be 4.

Question to test your memory: Why does line 20 in this program say INPUT A, while line 20 in the first program above said INPUT A$? If you've forgotten the difference, better go back and review Chapters 4 and 5.

4. If at First You Don't Succeed . . .

Using IF . . . THEN, you can program the computer to give a math test and check the answers. By adding GOTO, you can have the program tell you to keep trying till you get it right. Let's try it first with an easy problem:

```
NEW
1Ø PRINT "WHAT IS 2 + 2?"
2Ø INPUT A
3Ø IF A = 2 + 2 THEN PRINT "RIGHT!"
4Ø IF A <> 2 + 2 THEN PRINT "SORRY, TRY AGAIN": GOTO 1Ø
```

Notice that in lines 30 and 40 you don't have to tell the computer that the answer is 4. Remember that the computer always knows the answer to a math problem.

Run the program and see what happens when you get the problem wrong. Now change this program to make the problem harder.

5. Make It Hard or Easy.

You can make this type of program more interesting, and have the problems be as hard or easy as you want, if you change it like this:

```
NEW
1Ø PRINT "TYPE A NUMBER."
2Ø INPUT A
3Ø PRINT "TYPE ANOTHER NUMBER."
```

```
4Ø INPUT B
5Ø PRINT "WHAT IS THE SUM OF ";A;" AND ";B
6Ø INPUT C
7Ø IF C = A + B THEN PRINT "GOOD WORK":GOTO 1Ø
8Ø IF C <> A + B THEN PRINT "NO, TRY AGAIN" : GOTO 5Ø
```

Run this program till you are tired of it. (When you are ready to stop it, you'll have to break into it as you did with the program in Section 2 of this chapter.) After you see how this program works, list it and study the listing carefully to be sure you understand it.

Now change this program so you can use it to check you on your multiplication tables instead of on addition problems.

Note: Line 80 tells you what to do if you get the problem wrong (that is, **IF C<>A+B**). Actually, the only way you will get to line 80 is by typing in the wrong answer. If you get the problem right (line 70), the program goes back to line 10. So you can rewrite line 80 to be simply

```
8Ø PRINT "NO, TRY AGAIN": GOTO 5Ø
```

Using **IF** and **THEN** with **GOTO** allows your programs to branch in different directions. Think of your program as a map. An **IF . . . THEN** line represents a crossroad — a point where the computer must decide which way to go next. In this program **IF** you have the correct answer, **THEN** the computer chooses the road that takes you to a new problem. **IF** your answer is wrong, **THEN** the computer returns to the old problem to give you another chance to answer correctly.

6. A Variety of Choices.

You've seen how to use the equal sign (=) and the sign that means not equal to (<>) in programs with **IF** and **THEN**. You can also use the greater than > or less than < signs alone. For example, if you wanted to include only the numbers with "teen" in their names, you'd want every number greater than 12 and less than 20. That would be like line 40 in the program below.

You can also combine the equal sign with the greater or lesser sign. For example, this line

```
IF A<=1Ø THEN GOTO 5Ø
```

would mean "If A is 10 or any number smaller than 10, then go to line 50." (Some computers make you put the equal sign last in that combination; others don't care.)

Here's a program using some of these symbols in different ways:

```
NEW
1Ø PRINT "HOW OLD ARE YOU?"
2Ø INPUT A
3Ø IF A<=12 THEN PRINT "THAT'S AN AWESOME AGE!"
4Ø IF A>12 AND A <2Ø THEN PRINT "THAT'S A DYNAMITE AGE!"
5Ø IF A>=18 THEN PRINT "OLD ENOUGH TO VOTE!"
```

This program will give you one answer if you're 12 or younger, another answer if you're between 13 and 19, and a third answer if you're 18 or over. Try adding some lines to give it more answers for other ages.

7. Computing Alphabetical Order.

The symbols > and < can be used with words as well as numbers. The greater than > symbol will check not whether one word is bigger than another, but whether it comes afterward in alphabetical order. So this line:

```
IF A$>"PIZZA" THEN GOTO 1ØØ
```

means "If A$ is a word which would come after "pizza" in the dictionary, then go to line 100." And the less than < symbol, obviously, can check whether one word comes before another one in the dictionary. Here's a program:

```
NEW
1Ø PRINT "WHAT'S YOUR LAST NAME?"
2Ø INPUT N$
3Ø M$="MOUSE"
4Ø IF N$>M$ THEN PRINT "YOU'D COME AFTER MICKEY MOUSE IN THE
DICTIONARY."
```

```
5Ø IF N$<M$ THEN PRINT "YOU'D COME BEFORE MICKEY MOUSE IN
THE DICTIONARY."
6Ø IF N$=M$ THEN PRINT "OH, ARE YOU RELATED TO MICKEY MOUSE?"
```

Special Notes: Texas Instruments Computer

At this point the BASIC on the TI computer requires a different type of programming. You may not put two BASIC keywords in one line of a program on the TI. Any time you use **IF. . .THEN**, the word **THEN** must be followed by a line number. For example, in the first program in this chapter, you may not say

```
3Ø IF A$="YES" THEN PRINT "I LIKE YOU, TOO."
```

Instead you must write the program like this:

```
1Ø PRINT "DO YOU LIKE ME?"
2Ø INPUT A$
3Ø IF A$="YES" THEN 5Ø
4Ø IF A$= "NO" THEN 7Ø
5Ø PRINT "I LIKE YOU, TOO."
6Ø END
7Ø PRINT "YOU ARE A SNOB."
8Ø END
```

In addition, you cannot use a colon in a program line. Each line may have only one statement. So to fix that program to make it work for answers other than yes or no, add these lines:

```
45 PRINT "PLEASE TYPE YES OR NO."
46 GOTO 1Ø
```

The program in Section 3 would have to be rewritten like this:

```
1Ø PRINT "HOW MANY 3 CENT STAMPS IN A DOZEN?"
2Ø INPUT A
3Ø IF A=12 THEN 5Ø
4Ø IF A<>12 THEN 7Ø
5Ø PRINT "CORRECT"
```

```
60 END
70 PRINT "FOOLED YOU! THERE ARE ALWAYS 12 IN A DOZEN."
80 END
```

And in Section 4 the program would look like this:

```
10 PRINT "WHAT IS 2+2?"
20 INPUT A
30 IF A=2+2 THEN 50
40 IF A<>2+2 THEN 70
50 PRINT "RIGHT!"
60 END
70 PRINT "SORRY, TRY AGAIN."
80 GOTO 10
```

In other words, any time you use **IF. . .THEN** on the TI, you will have to write the program so that each **IF** sends the program to a certain line number. You must also be sure that you put in a line to tell the program when to end, or when to go on to another section, when you have finished with the **IF** part.

Special Notes: Timex Sinclair Computer

On the Timex Sinclair computer, when you see the BASIC word **THEN** in a program, you type it by pressing SHIFT 3.

Unlike the TI, the Timex Sinclair allows you to combine **IF. . .THEN** with other BASIC words. For example, you may say:

```
30 IF A$="YES" THEN PRINT "I LIKE YOU, TOO."
```

But, like the TI, the Timex Sinclair does *not* allow you to use the colon to combine two statements in one program line. On the Timex Sinclair, one possible way to write the program in Section 2 of this chapter is like this:

```
10 PRINT "DO YOU LIKE ME?"
20 INPUT A$
30 IF A$="YES" THEN PRINT "I LIKE YOU, TOO."
35 IF A$="YES" THEN STOP
```

```
4Ø IF A$="NO" THEN PRINT "YOU ARE A SNOB."
45 IF A$="NO" THEN STOP
5Ø PRINT "PLEASE TYPE YES OR NO."
6Ø GOTO 1Ø
```

Another possibility is this:

```
1Ø PRINT "DO YOU LIKE ME?"
2Ø INPUT A$
3Ø IF A$="YES" THEN GOTO 7Ø
4Ø IF A$="NO" THEN GOTO 9Ø
5Ø PRINT "PLEASE TYPE YES OR NO."
6Ø GOTO 1Ø
7Ø PRINT "I LIKE YOU, TOO"
8Ø STOP
9Ø PRINT "YOU ARE A SNOB."
1ØØ STOP
```

Note: The Timex Sinclair uses the word **STOP** instead of **END**. (Most other computers may use either **STOP** or **END**, but if you use **STOP**, the program ends with a **BREAK** message.) Also, the word **GOTO** after **THEN** in a line such as 30 is required on a Timex Sinclair while it is optional on most other computers.

With these two changes you may use the programs above for the TI or the Timex Sinclair.

From now on, if you are using a Timex Sinclair or a Texas Instruments computer, you must be aware of the peculiarities of their versions of BASIC. If you want to use the programs in the following chapters, you must rewrite many of them to avoid more than one BASIC statement in a line.

Practice 7

1. Write a program in which the computer asks someone what school he or she goes to. If the person answers with the name of your school, the computer

gives one reply. If the person answers with the name of any other school, the computer says something different.

2. Below is the beginning of a program to test your knowledge about computers. Read through the first five lines to be sure you understand how they work.

```
10 PRINT "THIS IS A QUIZ PROGRAM ABOUT COMPUTERS."
20 PRINT "WHAT IS THE NAME OF THE LANGUAGE FOR THIS COM-
PUTER?"
30 INPUT A$
40 IF A$="BASIC" THEN PRINT "RIGHT!"
50 IF A$<>"BASIC" THEN PRINT "NO, TRY THAT AGAIN.":GOTO 30
```

Now you add at least two more questions to this program about computers. Here are a couple of ideas, but you can use your own questions if you prefer. (We're not going to tell you the answers though. If you aren't sure, you'd better go back and start over again in Chapter 1.)

Sample questions to program:

1. A list of numbered instructions to the computer is called a _____."

2. What word tells the computer to start doing the program?

TI On the Texas Instruments computer, the program will have to look like this from line 40 on:

```
40 IF A$="BASIC" THEN 70
50 PRINT "NO, TRY AGAIN"
60 GOTO 20
70 PRINT "RIGHT!"
```

T/S The Timex Sinclair program could be essentially the same as the TI, except that you must add GOTO after THEN in line 70.

Answers to Practice 7

1. This is a sample program. Yours will be different, depending on the name of your school and the messages you choose to print.

10 PRINT "WHAT SCHOOL DO YOU GO TO?"

20 INPUT S$

30 IF S$="HARDY" THEN PRINT "THAT'S THE BEST!"

40 IF S$<>"HARDY" THEN PRINT "TOO BAD!"

Ʌ   Atari, add: 1 DIM S$ (20)

TI   On the TI, rewrite from line 30, like this:

30 IF S$="HARDY" THEN 50

40 IF S$<>"HARDY" THEN 70

50 PRINT "THAT'S THE BEST!"

60 END

70 PRINT "TOO BAD!"

2. These are the lines you should add using our sample questions:

60 PRINT "A LIST OF NUMBERED INSTRUCTIONS TO THE COMPUTER IS CALLED A _____."

70 INPUT A$

80 IF A$="PROGRAM" THEN PRINT "GOOD WORK!"

90 IF A$<>"PROGRAM" THEN PRINT "NO, THINK AGAIN.":GOTO 70

100 PRINT "WHAT WORD TELLS THE COMPUTER TO START DOING THE PROGRAM?"

110 INPUT A$

120 IF A$="RUN" THEN PRINT "EXCELLENT!"

130 IF A$<>"RUN" THEN PRINT "WRONG, PLEASE TRY AGAIN":GOTO 110

Ʌ   Atari, add: 1 DIM A$(15)

TI T/S Write the TI and Timex Sinclair programs following the style shown above in Practice section 2 for lines 40–70.

Note: It's all right to keep using A$ to stand for each different answer, since there's no need to have the computer remember the answer to the earlier questions once they're finished. In fact, it would only use up unnecessary memory space in the computer to create different string variable names for each answer.

8. Clean Up Your Act

In this chapter you'll learn how to get rid of some sloppy problems and make your programs look neat and professional.

1. Count Your Spaces.

You've probably noticed by now that the computer is pretty dumb about dividing words at the end of a line. Because it splits words in weird places, sometimes it's hard to read the messages on the screen. There's a very easy way to fix that, however, by simply putting some extra spaces in your typing to make your lines come out even.

Each brand of computer has a different number of spaces per line. For example, the Apple normally puts 40 letters or spaces on one line of the video screen. The TRS-80 Model I or III has 64 spaces to a line, but the TRS-80 Color Computer has only 32. The biggest letters and the shortest lines are found on the Commodore VIC 20, which can put only 22 letters on one line of the screen. We'll show you an example of how to adjust the spacing for the Apple. You can adapt it to the number of letter spaces per line on your computer.

Using the example of the last program in the Practice section of Chapter 7, you'll see that when you type line 20 in the program it comes out like this on the Apple's 40-character screen:

   🍎   ]2Ø PRINT "WHAT IS THE NAME OF THE LANGU
            AGE FOR THIS COMPUTER?"

When you run the program, that line comes on the screen looking like this:

   🍎   WHAT IS THE NAME OF THE LANGUAGE FOR THI
            S COMPUTER?

The easy way to keep the computer from breaking up words in funny places is just to keep your eye on the first quotation mark after the word **PRINT**. The letter after the first quote will be the beginning of the line on the screen. So when your typing comes around under the first quote, add spaces to make your words line up, like this:

   🍎   ]2Ø PRINT "WHAT IS THE NAME OF THE LANGU
            AGE FOR   THIS COMPUTER?"

Here's how the other **PRINT** lines in that program would look on the Apple when they are correctly spaced:

   🍎   ]6Ø PRINT "A LIST OF NUMBERED INSTRUCTION
            S TO THE   COMPUTER IS CALLED A ＿＿＿＿＿＿＿."
            ]1ØØ PRINT "WHAT WORD TELLS THE COMPUTER
            TO START   DOING THE PROGRAM?"

On the Commodore VIC 20 with only 22 characters per line, line 20 would look like this:

   ❡   2Ø PRINT "WHAT IS THE
  VIC   NAME OF THE LANGUAGE
              FOR THIS COMPUTER?"

The TRS-80 Model III, on the other hand, could put that whole question on one of its 64-character lines.

Retype that program, adjusting the spacing to fit the lines on your computer. (See the Answer section to Practice 7 for the complete program.)

2. A Pause to Refresh You.

After you have all the lines for that program correctly typed in, run it. Notice how the program prints the second question right away, as soon as you answer the first question correctly. It would be nicer if the computer would give you a chance to stop and catch your breath between questions.

You'll remember that the word to make the computer pause until the person hits RETURN (or ENTER) is INPUT. So you can put in an INPUT line to stop the program after each question. Then make the computer clear the screen, so it prints each question on a new "page."

To do this, you could insert a short routine like this after each question:

```
51 PRINT
52 PRINT "PRESS RETURN TO GO ON."
53 INPUT R$
54 (clear the screen)
```

Note: In Line 51, the word PRINT all by itself just makes the computer skip a line without printing anything on it. That spaces the program more attractively.

TRS   Line 52 on a TRS-80, TI, or Timex Sinclair should say

TI T/S   52 PRINT "PRESS ENTER TO GO ON."

Type these lines in and run the program to see how they work.

3. GOSUB . . . RETURN: A Round-Trip Ticket.

Now you can see the program stop in between the first and second question. To make it do that every time you ask a new question, you *could* type four lines like 51–54 after every question. But if your program ends up with 10 questions, that means you'd have to type those lines 9 times — and that's an awful lot of extra typing. (Also it uses up a lot of memory space on the computer.)

Fortunately, there is an easier way. You can make those lines into a *subroutine*.

Here's how a subroutine works. You take the lines you want to keep repeating over and over again. Instead of typing them in between each question, you put them way at the end of the program. (Let's say, we'll start at line 2000.) Then after every question is finished, you tell the computer to jump down to line 2000. There, it runs through the little routine of having you press

RETURN and clears the screen. Then it goes back up to print the next question, right where it left off.

The way to tell the computer to jump to line 2000 is this:

        GOSUB 2000

GOSUB is something like GOTO in that it makes the computer skip lines in the program. However, you might think of GOTO as a one-way ticket and GOSUB as a round trip.

Whenever you tell the computer to GOSUB, it must know when it has finished its little trip so it can jump back to the place it came from. In order to tell the computer to go back where it started, you type the word RETURN at the end of your subroutine. (For Apple, Atari, or Commodore computers, note that this is *not* the same as hitting the RETURN key. At the end of a subroutine, you type in the whole word RETURN.)

4. The Finished Product.

When you start writing longer programs, you'll often have many subroutines. It's a good idea to put one of those REM statements at the beginning of each subroutine to remind you what it's going to do.

So — here is the finished subroutine. Type it in. (Don't forget to use ENTER instead of RETURN in line 2020 but *not* in line 2050 on the TRS-80, TI, or Timex Sinclair):

        2000 REM CLEAR SCREEN BETWEEN QUESTIONS
        2010 PRINT
        2020 PRINT "PRESS RETURN TO GO ON."
        2030 INPUT R$
        2040 (clear the screen)
        2050 RETURN

5. Insert as Needed.

Now every time you want to use that routine, you just insert a line that says GOSUB 2000. In this program you want to put it after line 10 (which is the title of the program), then after line 50, after line 90, and after line 130, before you add another question. So you will type **GOSUB 2000** at lines 15, 55, 95, and 135. As you add more questions to the program, insert the **GOSUB 2000** line before you type each question. (You will also want to erase lines 51, 52, 53, and 54 since you won't need them anymore. If you've forgotten how to erase a line, look back to Chapter 2.)

Your program should now look more or less like this. (But if you have a Texas Instruments or Timex Sinclair, you must rewrite the **IF . . . THEN** routines as explained in Chapter 7. And don't forget the **DIM** line on the Atari.)

```
5 (clear the screen)
10 PRINT "THIS IS A QUIZ PROGRAM ABOUT COMPUTERS."
15 GOSUB 2000
20 PRINT "WHAT IS THE NAME OF THE LANGUAGE FOR THIS
COMPUTER?"
30 INPUT A$
40 IF A$="BASIC" THEN PRINT "RIGHT!"
50 IF A$<>"BASIC" THEN PRINT "NO, TRY THAT AGAIN.":GOTO 20
55 GOSUB 2000
60 PRINT "A LIST OF NUMBERED INSTRUCTIONS TO THE COMPUTER IS
CALLED A __ __ __ __ __ __ __."
70 INPUT A$
80 IF A$="PROGRAM" THEN PRINT "GOOD WORK!"
90 IF A$<>"PROGRAM" THEN PRINT "NO, THINK AGAIN.":GOTO 60
95 GOSUB 2000
100 PRINT "WHAT WORD TELLS THE COMPUTER TO START DOING THE
PROGRAM?"
110 INPUT A$
120 IF A$="RUN" THEN PRINT "EXCELLENT!"
130 IF A$<>"RUN" THEN PRINT "SORRY, PLEASE TRY AGAIN.":GOTO
100
135 GOSUB 2000
2000 REM CLEAR SCREEN BETWEEN QUESTIONS
```

```
2010 PRINT
2020 PRINT "PRESS RETURN TO GO ON."
2030 INPUT R$
2040 (clear the screen)
2050 RETURN
```

6. A Happy Ending.

When you have the GOSUB lines inserted and you run the program, you'll notice that there is one little bug in it. What error message do you get after you finish the program?

That error message happened because you haven't told the computer where you want to stop the program. List the program and you will see that right now the last line in the program is 2050 RETURN. The computer comes to the end of the program in the middle of a round trip. It wants to go back somewhere, but it has run out of lines and it has nowhere to go back to.

Fortunately, a BASIC program is different from a book or a movie. It doesn't have to end at the last line. You can tell the program to end anywhere you want just by putting in the word END (or on the Timex Sinclair, the word STOP). Since we want to end our program just before line 2000, we'll put in an END line right before that. Just type:

```
1990 END
```

7. Get Rid of Those Bugs.

When you think you have your program all set up correctly, the final step is to test it. First run the program, answering all the questions correctly. Then run it again giving wrong answers to the questions. Does the program behave the way you want it to? If not, don't worry. A program almost never comes out right the first time you run it. But it's almost always fixable. Just LIST and start debugging. If your program is too long to fit on the screen, you'll have to list just a portion at a time like this:

🍎 ⌨ TRS TI 🏃 LIST Ø-5Ø

LIST Ø,5Ø

If you have trouble finding the bug, check our Troubleshooting section at the end of the book (Appendix II).

8. GOSUB YES or GOSUB NO.

Any time you write a program that includes something you want to repeat more than two or three times, you should put that repeating part in a subroutine. Here's an example of another way to write that quiz program using more than one subroutine. Notice that you can go from one subroutine to another.

GOSUB 1ØØØ sends the computer to check whether your answer is correct. If it is correct, then GOSUB 2ØØØ prints YES in fancy letters. If it's not correct, then GOSUB 3ØØØ prints NO in fancy letters and gives you a choice: Do you want to try again, or do you want to see the answer? If you type "A", the program prints the answer (A$). If you type "T", you then return to the main part of the program for another chance. GOSUB 4ØØØ is the routine to clear the screen before starting a new question.

The illustration on page 98 shows you how to use graph paper to plan where to put the stars for the fancy letters. When you type in the subroutine, you may find it easier to follow the graph paper, so you can count the spaces. Once you get the idea, you can take a piece of graph paper and make your own designs to print on the computer. (On the other hand, if you don't want to bother with the fancy letters spelling YES and NO, just make up your own simpler right or wrong messages in subroutines 2000 and 3000.)

Here's the program. If you type it in, save it. We'll be using it again in Chapter 10.

```
NEW
5 (clear the screen)
1Ø PRINT "THIS IS A QUIZ PROGRAM ABOUT COMPUTERS."
15 GOSUB 4ØØØ
```

```
2Ø PRINT "WHAT IS THE NAME OF THE LANGUAGE FOR THIS
COMPUTER?"
3Ø A$ = "BASIC"
4Ø GOSUB 1ØØØ
45 IF B$="T" THEN 2Ø
5Ø PRINT "A LIST OF NUMBERED INSTRUCTIONS TO THE COMPUTER IS
CALLED A _ _ _ _ _ _ _ ."
6Ø A$="PROGRAM"
7Ø GOSUB 1ØØØ
75 IF B$="T" THEN 5Ø
8Ø PRINT "WHAT WORD TELLS THE COMPUTER TO START DOING THE
PROGRAM?"
9Ø A$="RUN"
1ØØ GOSUB 1ØØØ
1Ø5 IF B$="T" THEN 8Ø
11Ø PRINT "WHAT WORD SHOULD YOU TYPE BEFORE YOU BEGIN
WRITING A PROGRAM?"
12Ø A$="NEW"
13Ø GOSUB 1ØØØ
135 IF B$="T" THEN 11Ø
99Ø PRINT "THAT'S ALL!"
995 END
1ØØØ REM SUBROUTINE TO CHECK ANSWER
1Ø1Ø INPUT B$
1Ø2Ø IF B$=A$ THEN GOSUB 2ØØØ
1Ø3Ø IF B$<>A$ THEN GOSUB 3ØØØ
1Ø4Ø RETURN
```

97

1	2	3	4	5	6	7	8	9	10	11	12	13	14	15	16	17	18	19	20	21
X						X			X	X	X	X	X	X						
X	X					X			X					X						
X		X				X			X					X						
X			X			X			X					X						
X				X		X			X					X						
X					X	X			X					X						
X						X			X	X	X	X	X	X						
X						X			X	X	X	X	X			X	X	X	X	X
	X				X				X							X				X
		X		X					X							X				
			X						X	X	X	X				X	X	X	X	X
			X						X											X
			X						X							X				X
			X						X	X	X	X	X			X	X	X	X	X

```
2000 REM SUBROUTINE FOR RIGHT ANSWER
2010 PRINT   "*        *   *****  *****"
2020 PRINT   " *      *    *          *     *"
2030 PRINT   "  *   *      *          *      "
2040 PRINT   "    *        ****   *****"
2050 PRINT   "    *        *                *"
2060 PRINT   "    *        *          *    *"
2070 PRINT   "    *        *****  *****"
2080 GOSUB 4000
2090 RETURN
3000 REM SUBROUTINE FOR WRONG ANSWER
3010 PRINT   "*        *   ******"
3020 PRINT   "**       *   *        *"
3030 PRINT   "* *      *   *        *"
3040 PRINT   "*  *     *   *        *"
3050 PRINT   "*     *  *   *        *"
3060 PRINT   "*        ** *   *        *"
3070 PRINT   "*        *   ******"
3080 PRINT:PRINT "DO YOU WANT TO TRY AGAIN?"
3090 PRINT "TYPE T TO TRY AGAIN."
3100 PRINT "TYPE A TO SEE THE ANSWER."
3110 INPUT B$
3120 IF B$="A" THEN PRINT "THE ANSWER IS ";A$:GOSUB 4000
3130 (clear the screen)
3140 RETURN
4000 REM SUBROUTINE TO CLEAR SCREEN
4010 PRINT:PRINT:PRINT "PLEASE PRESS RETURN"
4020 INPUT R$
4030 (clear the screen)
4040 RETURN
```

Remember: Use **ENTER** in line 4010, instead of **RETURN** if you

TRS   have a "T" computer (TRS-80, TI, or Timex Sinclair). And for the TI and

TI   Timex Sinclair, you must rewrite any lines that include a colon. The TI
T/S   must also use a special IF . . . THEN format explained in Chapter 7. And the
Timex Sinclair uses STOP instead of END (line 995).

This program uses subroutines to save you from typing those IF . . . THEN lines after every question. Every time you ask a new question you change the variable A$ to equal the correct answer. The subroutine 1000–1030 checks to see whether the answer typed in for INPUT equals the value of A$ at that moment. If it does, then it goes to the YES subroutine beginning at 2000. If the answer was wrong, it goes to the subroutine at 3000 to print NO. Next you may choose whether to try again or see the answer. Lines 4000–4040 are the familiar clear the screen routine.

Try adding a few of your own questions to this program to be sure you understand how it works.

Practice 8

1. Add at least three more questions to the quiz program on computers that you started in Practice 7. When you have finished, debug the program to make sure all these problems are taken care of:
- Are all your PRINT lines typed correctly so that words don't get split in funny places when you run the program?
- Did you remember to call up the subroutine to make the program clear the screen between every question?
- Did you run the program with right answers and wrong answers to make sure it works correctly both ways?
2. Write your own quiz program about a subject you have studied in school or about something you have learned on your own. Or maybe you would like to use tricky questions or brain teasers. (See the program QWERT in Section 1 of Chapter 12 for an example of that type.)

No answers are given to the practice problems in this chapter. The correct answers will come from you when you have finished and debugged your programs. Any program that works the way you want it to is right!

9.

Make Your Computer a Gambler

So far in your programming with variables, you have told the computer exactly what to do. You have made X=8, or you have made N$="NANCY". But sometimes — for example, when you are playing a game — you want the computer to decide what to do.

Suppose you wanted to program a game that involved guessing a number. It wouldn't be much fun if you already knew the number before you started. What you want to do is to make the computer pick a number at *random*. A random number is like what you get when you roll dice, or pick a card, or toss a coin. You can make the computer pretend to do any of those things with the function RND.

1. Random Fractions.

The RND function will make the computer pick a random number between 0 and 1. Here's how it works on different computers:

On the Apple, Atari, and Commodore computers, you type

   ♣ C= PRINT RND(1)

On the TI and Timex Sinclair you type

  TI T/S PRINT RND

Note: On the Timex Sinclair you get RND by typing SHIFT ENTER T

On the TRS-80 you type

TRS   PRINT RND(Ø)

Type it several times. Each time the computer will print a different decimal fraction between 0 and 1. You can put it in a program, like this

🍎 人 Ⴀ NEW
       1Ø PRINT RND(1)
       2Ø GOTO 1Ø

TI T/S NEW
       1Ø PRINT RND
       2Ø GOTO 1Ø

TRS   NEW
       1Ø PRINT RND(Ø)
       2Ø GOTO 1Ø

and you will see the computer print a whole string of different random numbers.

2. Round Off Your Randoms.

Usually, however, you don't want to have decimal fractions in a program with random numbers. For example, if you want the computer to pretend to roll dice, you want it to pick at random a *whole* number between 1 and 6. The TRS-80 computer makes it very easy to do this, because it automatically rounds off when you put a number 1 or larger in the parentheses after RND.

Most other microcomputers don't automatically round off, so you have to go through a somewhat more elaborate routine to make them print a useful random number. To get a random number between 1 and 6, on the Apple, Atari, or Commodore computers, for example, you would use this formula:

🍎 人 Ⴀ NEW
       1Ø R = INT(RND(1) * 6) + 1
       2Ø PRINT R

On the TI or Timex Sinclair, type:

TI T/S NEW

```
10 LET R = INT (RND*6) + 1
20 PRINT R
```

(You don't have to use R. Any other letter would work just as well.)

This formula tells the computer to pick a random whole number between 1 and 6. INT stands for **INTEGER**, which means "whole number." The term INT makes the computer round off the number. (Actually, it always rounds down to the smaller number. That's why you have to add 1 at the end. If you don't add 1, you get a number between 0 and 5.)

To translate that formula into English you might say: (RND(1) * 6) + 1 means: pick a random number between 0 and 1 and multiply it times 6. Then add 1 to that number. INT means: drop off anything after the decimal point so your final answer is a whole number.

3. Computer Dice.

The TRS-80 can use that same INT formula, although you must say RND(Ø) instead of RND(1). But the TRS-80 also has a much easier way to do it. The simplest way to make the TRS-80 computer print a random number between 1 and 6 is this:

TRS
```
NEW
10 RANDOM: R = RND(6)
20 PRINT R
```

(The RANDOM command makes the computer keep changing the random numbers.)

On other computers use the function described in Section 2:

 NEW
```
10 R=INT(RND(1)*6)+1
20 PRINT R
```

TI T/S
```
NEW
10 LET R = INT (RND*6) + 1
20 PRINT R
```

103

Type in the program for your computer and run it a few times. Each time you should get a different number between 1 and 6, just like rolling a die. (You can add the line

       30 GOTO 10

if you want to make the computer keep on rolling the die over and over.)

If you want to roll a pair of dice, you will need two variables. Add this line to your program:

   妖 C⁼ 15 L=INT(RND(1)*6)+1

  TI T/S 15 LET L=INT(RND*6)+1

  TRS   15 L=RND(6)

Now change line 30 to read:

       30 PRINT L,R

4. Change the Ceiling.

To get a random number between 1 and 100 just change the number you use to multiply, like this:

   妖 C⁼ R=INT(RND(1)*100)+1

  TI T/S LET R=INT(RND*100)+1

  TRS   R=RND(100)

Practice. Make the computer pick a random number between 1 and 52, 1 and 333, 1 and 1000, or any range you choose.

5. Change the Floor.

You don't have to make your random numbers start with 1. Suppose you want to pick a random number between 10 and 20. Here's how to do that with the INT formula:

   妖 C⁼ R=INT(RND(1) * 11) + 10

  TI T/S LET R=INT(RND*11) + 10

The last number in that formula (10) tells the computer where to start counting for the random numbers. The number just before that (11) tells it how many numbers to count. (If you count on your fingers, starting with 10 and ending with 20, you will see that you count 11 numbers.)

The rule to remember is: Take the high number (we'll call it H), subtract the low number (L), and add 1. That number (H−L+1) is what you put after the * sign in the **RND** formula. At the end insert the low number (L) after the + sign.

You can see how this works in the example above: (H−L+1) is the same as (20−10+1) or 11. Here's how it looks written out in math terms as you might use it in a program:

  🍎 ㆆ Ꮹ R=INT(RND(1) * (H−L+1)) + L

  TI T/S LET R=INT(RND * (H−L+1)) + L

This may seem like a very involved formula, but you don't have to memorize it! Just remember where to look it up when you want to use it, then copy it into your program. And don't get confused by all those parentheses. You have to have them there to make the computer do the arithmetic correctly. Remember that parentheses come in pairs ( ), and the above formula has three pairs.

On the TRS-80 you pick a random number between 10 and 20 like this:

  TRS   R=RND(11)+9

The formula is this:

        R=RND(H−L+1) + L−1

You could actually put those lines in a program like this:

```
NEW
10 PRINT "THIS PROGRAM WILL PRINT A SERIES OF RANDOM
NUMBERS IN ANY RANGE YOU CHOOSE."
20 PRINT "TYPE THE LOW NUMBER."
30 INPUT L
40 PRINT "TYPE THE HIGH NUMBER."
50 INPUT H
```

  🍎 ㆆ Ꮹ 60 R=INT(RND(1) * (H−L+1)) + L

  TI T/S 60 LET R=INT(RND * (H−L+1)) + L

TRS   6Ø RANDOM: R=RND(H—L+1)+L—1

70 PRINT R
80 GOTO 6Ø

You can also use that formula to plug in your numbers when you write a program for a certain purpose. For example, suppose you want to write a program in which the computer will predict how old a person will be when he or she gets married. We'll pick 16 as the lower age limit and 60 as the higher age. So you can write a little routine like this:

NEW

🍎 🜋 ⊂ 1Ø A=INT(RND(1) * (60—16+1)) + 16

TI T/S 1Ø LET A=INT(RND * (6Ø—16+1)) + 16

TRS   1Ø RANDOM: A=RND(60—16+1) + 15

2Ø PRINT "TYPE YOUR NAME."
3Ø INPUT N$
4Ø PRINT "THE COMPUTER PREDICTS THAT "
5Ø PRINT N$;" WILL MARRY AT AGE ";A

🜋   For Atari, add the DIM line: 1 DIM N$(2Ø)

If you wanted to go to the trouble, you could do the math in line 10 or 11 yourself. But why should you bother to figure out that (60—16+1) equals 45 when the computer will do it for you much quicker than you can? Also, if you leave the numbers written out, it's easy to see at a glance exactly where the random numbers will begin and end.

6. Computer Coin Toss.

When the computer picks a random number, it doesn't have to print the number. You can tell it to print something else — like heads or tails. Here's a program to make the computer pretend to be flipping a coin.

```
        NEW
♦ ٨ ⌒  1Ø C=INT(RND(1) *2) + 1


TI  T/S  1Ø LET C = INT(RND * 2) + 1


TRS     1Ø RANDOM: C=RND(2)


        2Ø IF C=1 THEN PRINT "HEADS"
        3Ø IF C=2 THEN PRINT "TAILS"
        4Ø GOTO 1Ø
```

Run that program and watch the computer flip out.

7. Better than a Crystal Ball.

You can write programs using the RND function with various kinds of INPUT to make your computer pretend to be a fortuneteller. Here's an example:

```
        NEW
        1Ø PRINT "I'LL PREDICT THE WINNER OF THE GAME."
        2Ø PRINT "TYPE THE NAME OF ONE TEAM."
        3Ø INPUT A$
        4Ø PRINT "THE OTHER TEAM?"
        5Ø INPUT B$


♦ ٨ ⌒  6Ø T=INT(RND(1)*2)+1


TI  T/S  6Ø LET T=INT(RND*2)+1


TRS     6Ø RANDOM: T=RND(2)


        7Ø PRINT "THE COMPUTER'S PREDICTION IS:"
        8Ø IF T=1 THEN PRINT A$;" WILL WIN."
        9Ø IF T=2 THEN PRINT B$;" WILL WIN."
```

♄   On the Atari, add this line: **1 DIM A$(3Ø), B$(3Ø)**

TI   On the TI, adjust the IF...THEN routines as explained in Chapter 7.

Here's a sample of what that program might look like when you run it. (We've put the **INPUT** that the person types in italics.)

```
I'LL PREDICT THE WINNER OF THE GAME.
TYPE THE NAME OF ONE TEAM.
? RED SOX
THE OTHER TEAM?
? YANKEES
THE COMPUTER'S PREDICTION IS:
RED SOX WILL WIN.
```

In that program the computer is doing exactly the same thing you would do if you flipped a coin, saying "Heads it'll be Red Sox, tails it'll be Yankees." But somehow it seems much more official when you get the computer to say it! Then, too, if you bet and lose, you can always blame it on the computer.

Practice. Can you add a routine to that program to make it print a random prediction for the score? Since baseball teams rarely score more than 20 runs a game, make the range between 0 and 20. (If you get stuck, look for the solution in the Answer section for this chapter.)

8. Play Guess My Number.

One of the most popular simple games you can program using the random number picker is Hi-Lo, or Guess My Number. Here's one version of that program, along with a sample RUN. Type it in and have fun!

```
NEW
1Ø (clear the screen)
2Ø PRINT "I'LL PICK A SECRET NUMBER BETWEEN ANY TWO NUMBERS
YOU CHOOSE."
3Ø PRINT "YOU TRY TO GUESS MY NUMBER."
4Ø PRINT "TYPE THE LOW NUMBER."
5Ø INPUT L
```

```
6Ø PRINT "TYPE THE HIGH NUMBER."
7Ø INPUT H
```

🍎 🙏 ℂ⹁ `8Ø R–INT(RND(1) * (H–L+1)) + L`

TRS `8Ø RANDOM: R=RND(H–L+1)+L–1`

```
9Ø PRINT "OKAY. GUESS MY SECRET NUMBER BETWEEN ";L;" AND ";H
1ØØ INPUT G
11Ø IF G > R THEN PRINT "YOUR GUESS WAS TOO HIGH. TRY
AGAIN.":GOTO 1ØØ
12Ø IF G < R THEN PRINT "YOUR GUESS WAS TOO LOW. TRY
AGAIN.":GOTO 1ØØ
13Ø IF G=R THEN PRINT "YOU GOT IT!!! DO YOU WANT TO PLAY AGAIN?
TYPE Y FOR YES OR N FOR NO."
14Ø INPUT A$
15Ø IF A$="Y" THEN GOTO 1Ø
16Ø IF A$="N" THEN PRINT "OKAY. BYE!":END
17Ø PRINT "PLEASE TYPE Y OR N.":GOTO 14Ø
```

🙏   On the Atari, add line 1: `1 DIM A$(1Ø)`

For the TI and Timex Sinclair, change the program like this, beginning with line 80. (Remember on the Timex Sinclair to use **GOTO** after every **THEN** and **STOP** instead of **END**.)

TI T/S `8Ø LET R= INT(RND*(H–L+1))+L`

```
9Ø PRINT "OKAY. GUESS MY SECRET NUMBER BETWEEN ";L;" AND ";H
1ØØ INPUT G
11Ø IF G>R THEN 2ØØ
12Ø IF G<R THEN 3ØØ
13Ø PRINT "YOU GOT IT! PLAY AGAIN? TYPE Y OR N."
14Ø INPUT A$
15Ø IF A$="Y" THEN 1Ø
16Ø IF A$="N" THEN 4ØØ
```

```
17Ø PRINT "PLEASE TYPE Y OR N."
18Ø GOTO 14Ø
2ØØ PRINT "YOUR GUESS WAS TOO HIGH. TRY AGAIN."
21Ø GOTO 1ØØ
3ØØ PRINT "YOUR GUESS WAS TOO LOW. TRY AGAIN."
31Ø GOTO 1ØØ
4ØØ PRINT "OKAY. BYE!"
41Ø END
```

Here's a sample run:

```
RUN
I'LL PICK A SECRET NUMBER BETWEEN ANY TWO NUMBERS YOU
CHOOSE.
YOU TRY TO GUESS MY NUMBER.
TYPE THE LOW NUMBER.
? 1
TYPE THE HIGH NUMBER.
? 1ØØ
OKAY. GUESS A NUMBER BETWEEN 1 AND 1ØØ.
? 5Ø
YOUR GUESS WAS TOO LOW. TRY AGAIN.
? 75
YOUR GUESS WAS TOO LOW. TRY AGAIN.
? 9Ø
YOUR GUESS WAS TOO HIGH. TRY AGAIN.
? 8Ø
YOUR GUESS WAS TOO HIGH. TRY AGAIN.
? 77
YOUR GUESS WAS TOO LOW. TRY AGAIN.
? 78
YOU GOT IT!!! DO YOU WANT TO PLAY
AGAIN? TYPE Y FOR YES OR N FOR NO.
? MAYBE
```

PLEASE TYPE Y OR N.
? *N*
OKAY. BYE!

Practice 9

1. Write a program to choose the following random numbers:

> A number between 2 and 50
>
> A number between 50 and 550
>
> A number between 0 and 24

2. Use the random number formulas from Problem 1 to write a program to tell a person's fortune. The first number will tell how many years from now the person will get married. The second number tells how much he/she will weigh then. The third number tells how many children he/she will have. Here's a sample run. You write the program.

> TELL ME YOUR NAME AND I WILL TELL YOU YOUR FORTUNE.
>
> ? *GEORGE*
>
> GEORGE WILL GET MARRIED 25 YEARS FROM NOW.
>
> AT THAT TIME GEORGE WILL WEIGH 395 POUNDS.
>
> THE NUMBER OF CHILDREN GEORGE WILL HAVE IS 13.

3. Write a program to make the computer pretend to pick a card at random from a deck. (In order to keep the program simple, we'll use 1 for Ace and 11, 12, 13 for Jack, Queen, King.) Here are some of the steps you will go through:

First, make the computer pick a random number between 1 and 13 to stand for the card number.

Then make it pick a random number between 1 and 4 to stand for the suit (hearts, diamonds, clubs, or spades).

Finally, make the computer print the number and the suit of the card.

Answers to Practice 9

Answer to practice problem in Section 5 of Chapter 9:

```
 ❤ 人 C=  100 A=INT(RND (1) * 21)
            110 B=INT(RND (1) * 21)


   TI  T/S  100 LET A=INT(RND * 21)
            110 LET B=INT(RND * 21)


   TRS      100 RANDOM: A=RND(21)−1
            110 B=RND(21)−1


            120 IF A =< B THEN GOTO 100
            130 PRINT "THE SCORE WILL BE ";A;"−";B
```

Note: This program will print a score for each team somewhere between 0 and 20 — a reasonable range for baseball. Obviously, you'd change the range upward for basketball or downward for soccer. Line 120 makes sure the first number that the computer predicts in the score will be higher than the second score. It tells the computer: If you pick a number for A that is equal to or less than B, then pick again.

Answers to Exercises in Practice 9:

1.

```
            10 M=INT(RND(1) * (50−2+1)) + 2
 ❤ 人 C=  20 W=INT(RND(1) * (550−50+1)) + 50
            30 C=INT(RND(1) * 25)


            10 LET M=INT(RND * (50−2+1)) + 2
   TI  T/S  20 LET W=INT(RND * (550−50+1))+50
            30 LET C=INT(RND * 25)


            10 RANDOM: M=RND(50−2+1)+1
   TRS      20 W=RND(550−50+1)+49
            30 C=RND(25)−1
```

2. Add these lines to the program in Problem 1:

```
4Ø PRINT "WHAT IS YOUR NAME?"
5Ø INPUT N$
6Ø PRINT N$;" WILL GET MARRIED ";M;" YEARS FROM NOW."
7Ø PRINT "AT THAT TIME ";N$;" WILL WEIGH ";W;" POUNDS."
8Ø PRINT "THE NUMBER OF CHILDREN ";N$;" WILL HAVE IS ";C
```

Ѧ   Atari, add line: 1 DIM A$(20)

3. Answer to card problem:

 Ѧ ☾
```
1Ø C=INT(RND (1) * 13) + 1
2Ø S=INT(RND (1) * 4) + 1
```

TI   T/S
```
1Ø LET C=INT(RND * 13) + 1
2Ø LET S = INT(RND * 4) + 1
```

TRS
```
1Ø RANDOM: C=RND(13)
2Ø S=RND(4)

3Ø IF S=1 THEN S$="HEARTS"
4Ø IF S=2 THEN S$="DIAMONDS"
5Ø IF S=3 THEN S$="CLUBS"
6Ø IF S=4 THEN S$="SPADES"
7Ø PRINT "THE COMPUTER'S CARD IS "
8Ø PRINT C;" OF ";S$
```

TI   Rewrite the IF. . .THEN lines for the TI.

10.
You Can Count on Your Computer

Counting is one of the things a computer does best. To tell the computer to count, you use the words **FOR** and **NEXT**, with a variable letter.

1. Count to 100.

You tell the computer to count to 100 with a program like this:

```
10 FOR N = 1 TO 100
20 NEXT N
```

That just tells the computer to count to itself. To make it "count out loud" you have to tell it to PRINT the numbers, like this:

```
10 FOR N=1 TO 100
15 PRINT N
20 NEXT N
RUN
```

Type that program and watch the numbers roll by.

Note: On the Timex Sinclair the counting will stop as soon as the screen fills up. Press **CONT** to make it continue.

The letter **N**, you will remember, is a *variable,* which means it can change. Every time the computer printed a new number from 1 to 100 it was changing **N** to stand for that number.

114

2. Counting Words.

The computer can count words, too. Let's make it count to 10. But instead of showing us the numbers 1 to 10, let's make it print **HELLO** 10 times. Here's the program:

```
NEW
1Ø FOR H = 1 TO 1Ø
2Ø PRINT "HELLO"
3Ø NEXT H
```

Run that program and count the hellos. Counting in BASIC can seem a little confusing till you get the hang of it. In the next section we'll go through the process step by step to explain how it works.

3. Loop the Loop.

FOR and **NEXT** *always* go together in a program. Think of **FOR** as one end of a rope and **NEXT** as the other end. Everything between them is inside a *loop*.

In the **FOR** line you tell the computer how many times to go around the loop. If you say **FOR A = 1 TO 1Ø**, the computer will go around the loop 10 times. Everything between **FOR** and **NEXT** will get done 10 times.

You can understand this if you pretend to be the computer, making a **FOR** . . . **NEXT** loop. Draw a line on a piece of paper. Write FOR at one end of the line and NEXT at the other end.

```
┌FOR
│
│
└NEXT
```

Now decide how many times you want to go between FOR and NEXT. We'll let T stand for the number of trips. If you decide to make 6 trips you write:

```
FOR T = 1 TO 6



NEXT T
```

Each time you make a trip from FOR to NEXT, you will do everything that comes along the line. So let's add an activity.

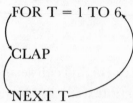

```
FOR T = 1 TO 6


CLAP


NEXT T
```

Imagine you are walking between FOR and NEXT. Every time you pass CLAP, you must clap your hands. When you come to NEXT, you turn around and jump back to FOR until you've used up all your trips. When you count 6 claps, you can stop, or go on to do something else.

Here's how to write that in a computer program. (Since the computer can't clap, we'll make it print the word "clap.")

```
1Ø FOR T = 1 TO 6
2Ø PRINT "CLAP"
3Ø NEXT T
```

Run that program to see the computer give you 6 claps.

When we gave you those instructions, we didn't tell you to count out loud. You should have been keeping count silently in your head. To tell you to count out loud in English, we might add something like this:

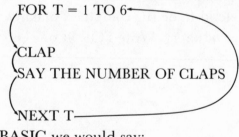

```
FOR T = 1 TO 6


CLAP
SAY THE NUMBER OF CLAPS


NEXT T
```

In BASIC we would say:

```
1Ø FOR T = 1 TO 6
```

```
20 PRINT "CLAP"
30 PRINT T
40 NEXT T
RUN
```

When you tell the computer to print T, you are just telling it to count "out loud" so we can see the numbers.

4. FOR the NEXT Time You Get in Trouble.

Did you ever get in trouble with your teacher and have to write something like "I will not talk in class" 25 times? Here's a nice little program to let the computer do the work and save you from writer's cramp.

```
NEW
10 A$ = "I WILL NOT TALK IN CLASS."
20 FOR N = 1 TO 25
30 PRINT N;A$
40 NEXT N
```

ᴧ   For Atari, add: 1 DIM A$(50)

The handy thing about that program is that you can easily change it when you get into a different kind of trouble. Just change line 10 to:

```
10 A$ = "I WILL REMEMBER MY HOMEWORK."
```

or

```
10 A$ = "I WILL NOT CHEW GUM IN SCHOOL."
```

or whatever.

5. Program a Pause.

Sometimes you will want to use FOR . . . NEXT not to make the computer print something but just to slow it down for a few seconds. Type this program:

```
NEW
10 (clear the screen)
20 PRINT "WHAT'S YOUR NAME?"
```

```
30 INPUT N$
40 PRINT "HELLO"
50 PRINT N$
```

🔺   For Atari, add: 1 DIM N$(20)

Run that program once. Then add these lines:

```
45 FOR A = 1 TO 600
46 NEXT A
```

Now run the program again. Do you see how the computer pauses in between Hello and your name? That's because you told it to stop and count to 600 before it went on. (You can see how fast the computer counts when you realize it's going from 1 to 600 in that second or so.) Try changing the 600 to higher and lower numbers to see longer and shorter pauses.

Each computer counts at a different rate of speed. The Apple and the Commodore count the fastest, followed by the Atari and TRS-80. Significantly slower is the Texas Instruments, and the real tortoise of the group is the Timex Sinclair. In fact, you will probably want to change the 600 in line 45 to a smaller number for the Timex Sinclair because you'll get bored waiting for it to finish counting.

Now add this line

```
60 GOTO 45
```

to see the computer print your name with rhythm.

6. Put Your Name in Lights.

Instead of filling up the screen with your name, let's make it flash on and off like a neon sign.

Break into the program and add these lines:

```
51 FOR A = 1 TO 300
52 NEXT A
53 (clear the screen)
```

These lines make the computer erase the screen and count again before it prints your name, so it looks as though your name is flashing.

7. Keep Those Loops Nested.

One thing to watch out for in a program with more than one FOR ... NEXT loop is not to get your loops tangled. Programmers say your loops have to be *nested.* Here's how it works.

Imagine some instructions like this: Jump 5 times. After each jump clap 3 times. You're counting two separate things — jumps and claps — so you need to keep track of each thing separately. If you're a computer you need two FOR ... NEXT loops like this:

```
NEW
10 FOR J = 1 TO 5
20 PRINT "JUMP";J
30 FOR C = 1 TO 3
40 PRINT "CLAP";C
50 NEXT C
60 NEXT J
RUN
```

Notice how the CLAP or C loop is nested *inside* the JUMP or J loop. Just to see what will happen if you do it wrong, switch lines 50 and 60 like this:

```
50 NEXT J
60 NEXT C
```

When you try to run that program you'll get an error message. If you look at the imaginary lines connecting your FOR ... NEXT variables now, you'll see that they're tangled up:

```
10 FOR J = 1 TO 5
20 PRINT "JUMP";J
30 FOR C = 1 TO 3
40 PRINT "CLAP";C
50 NEXT J
60 NEXT C
RUN
```

The computer runs out of its 5 jumps while it's still trying to do claps, so you get a NEXT WITHOUT FOR error. Any time you see that error message in a program, you should go back and trace your loops so you can untangle them.

8. Stepping Up or Down.

Your computer can also count by twos, threes, fives, nines, or any other number. Or it can count backward. To make it do those tricks, you add the word STEP in the FOR . . . NEXT loop. Here's how to make the computer print the 9 times table, for example:

```
NEW
1Ø FOR X=Ø TO 1Ø8 STEP 9
2Ø PRINT X
3Ø NEXT X
```

When you run that program, you'll see every number in the nines table from 0 times 9 to 12 times 9. STEP 9 just tells the computer to count by nines.

Here's how to make the computer count backward, like a rocket countdown:

```
NEW
1Ø FOR X=1Ø TO Ø STEP −1
2Ø PRINT X
3Ø NEXT X
4Ø PRINT "BLASTOFF!!"
```

You can add a few lines to that program to make the computer actually act like a rocket ship. Type these lines:

```
25 FOR T = 1 TO 2ØØ
26 NEXT T
5Ø PRINT
6Ø GOTO 5Ø
```

Line 25 creates a pause between the numbers as it counts down. Lines 50 and 60 move the printing up and off the screen so it actually seems to take off into space. (Don't forget to press BREAK, RUN/STOP, CTRL C, or FCTN 4 to get yourself out of the line 50–60 loop and back in control.)

9. How Fast Are You?

Here is a program using FOR . . . NEXT loops to test your reflexes. Try this with your friends to see who can get the fastest time.

T/S   *Note:* This program is not recommended for a Timex Sinclair because
TI   the computer counts too slowly. It will work on a Texas Instruments, but not as well as on a faster computer.

```
NEW
5 (clear the screen)
10 PRINT "THIS PROGRAM WILL TEST YOUR REACTION TIME."
20 PRINT:PRINT "WAIT TILL YOU SEE THE WORD 'GO'."
30 PRINT "AFTER YOU SEE 'GO' PRESS"
```

人 TRS
```
40 PRINT "THE BREAK KEY"
```

C=
```
40 PRINT "THE RUN/STOP KEY"
```

🍎
```
40 PRINT "THE CTRL KEY AND C"
```

TI
```
40 PRINT "THE FCTN KEY AND 4"
```

```
50 PRINT "AS QUICKLY AS YOU CAN."
60 PRINT:PRINT "THE SMALLER THE LAST NUMBER YOU SEE ON THE
SCREEN"
70 PRINT "THE FASTER YOU ARE."
80 PRINT:PRINT "NOW PRESS RETURN AND WAIT FOR 'GO.' "
90 INPUT R$
100 REM PICK RANDOM NUMBER FOR TIME DELAY
```

🍎 人 C=
```
110 R=INT(RND(1)*6000) + 1
```

TI
```
110 R=INT(RND*2000)+1
```

```
TRS     11Ø RANDOM:R=RND(3ØØØ)

        12Ø FOR X = 1 TO R
        121 NEXT X
        13Ø PRINT "GO"
        14Ø FOR T=1 TO 1ØØØ
        15Ø PRINT T
        16Ø NEXT T
```

The first several lines of that program are the instructions. If you just want to see how the program works, start typing at line 110. Then when you type RUN, wait for GO. As soon as you see GO, hit BREAK (or the equivalent for your computer). The number you see will be your reaction time (though it's measured in "computer time," not in seconds).

Here's an explanation of some of the lines:

- Line 110 picks a random number. (Since the TRS-80 and TI count slower than the other computers, we've given them a lower range to pick from.)
- Line 120 tells the computer to count up to that random number before it goes on. (We want a random number so you won't be able to guess how long it's going to take before you see GO.)
- Lines 130–160: The program prints GO and starts counting. The time it takes you between seeing GO and hitting BREAK is your reaction time.

10. Fancy Footwork and Frowning Faces.

A fun way to use FOR . . . NEXT loops is to make pictures that seem to move on the screen. Here are two animated programs — one to create a little dancing figure and the other to make a face that goes from calm to angry. They may give you some ideas for your own animations.

Note: On the TRS-80 these pictures won't look quite as good because the TRS-

TRS   80 leaves more space between its lines. This makes the pictures look less connected.

TI   These programs are not recommended for the Texas Instruments, because it prints at the bottom of the screen. This placement keeps the

T/S   animation from working properly. They also will not work well on a Timex Sinclair because of its slow processor.

Note: In lines 20 and 70, type a space *before* the O. In lines 40 and 90, type a space between the two characters.

```
NEW
5 REM PRINTS DANCING FIGURE
1Ø (clear the screen)
2Ø PRINT " O "
3Ø PRINT "/X>"
4Ø PRINT "( )"
5Ø FOR T=1 TO 3ØØ:NEXT T
6Ø (clear the screen)
7Ø PRINT " O "
8Ø PRINT "−X)"
9Ø PRINT "/ >"
1ØØ FOR T =1 TO 3ØØ:NEXT T
11Ø GOTO 1Ø
```

That program prints the first figure for a short time. Then it clears the screen and prints a second figure directly on top of the first, with its arms and legs in a slightly different position. By going back and forth between the two, the program makes the little person seem to dance. You may want to adjust the numbers in the **FOR** . . . **NEXT** lines to make the figure dance faster or slower.

And here's the program to print the face:

```
NEW
5 (clear the screen)
1Ø PRINT   "((((((((("
2Ø PRINT   "---------"
3Ø PRINT   "!         !"
4Ø PRINT   "! =    = !"
5Ø PRINT   "! Ø    Ø !"
6Ø PRINT   "!         !"
7Ø PRINT   "!    V    !"
8Ø PRINT   "!         !"
9Ø PRINT   "!  (---)  !"
1ØØ PRINT "!         !"
11Ø PRINT "---------"
12Ø FOR T=1 TO 4ØØ:NEXT T
13Ø (clear the screen)
14Ø PRINT "/////////"
15Ø PRINT "---------"
16Ø PRINT "!         !"
17Ø PRINT "! =)  (= !"
18Ø PRINT "! @    @!"
19Ø PRINT "!         !"
2ØØ PRINT "!    V    !"
21Ø PRINT "!         !"
22Ø PRINT "!  (VVV)  !"
23Ø PRINT "!         !"
24Ø PRINT "---------"
25Ø FOR T= TO 4ØØ:NEXT T
26Ø GOTO 5
```

/

11. Some Notes on Graphics.

If you have an Atari or a Commodore PET or VIC you can make lots of fancier pictures than these by using the special graphics characters on each key. (See the notes on Special Keys in Chapter 1 for more information on these.)

The Apple, Atari, Texas Instruments, and TRS-80 also have different ways you can go about making pictures on the screen by following the special rules for each computer. Since these rules are so different for each type of machine, we're not going to go into them here. You'll probably want to read other books to explore the graphics possibilities for your own computer.

Just about anything you do with computer graphics will involve FOR . . . NEXT loops. So by the time you've written enough FOR . . . NEXT programs to understand how that command works you should be ready to start programming your own graphics.

12. Keeping Score.

We've seen a lot of different programs using FOR . . . NEXT to make the computer count. Another way to make the computer count is with a line like this in a program:

        C = C + 1

At first that may seem like nonsense. If C, for example, equals 5, then how can 5 equal 5 + 1? But an equal sign in a BASIC program is not the same as an equal sign in a math problem. In math whatever you put on the left side of the equal sign has to add up to exactly the same number as what's on the right side. In BASIC an equal sign tells the computer to change whatever is on the left side to *make* it equal what's on the right side.

Remember that C is a *variable:* it changes. The line C = C + 1 actually means to the computer: Change C by adding one more to it. If the old C was 5, change the new C into 6. Here's a silly little program to show you how this works:

```
NEW
1Ø PRINT C
2Ø PRINT "HI"
3Ø C=C+1
35 PRINT C
4Ø PRINT "HO"
5Ø C=C+1
55 PRINT C
6Ø PRINT "HA"
7Ø C=C+1
75 PRINT C
8Ø PRINT "HEE HEE"
9Ø C=C+1
95 PRINT C
1ØØ PRINT "THAT MAKES ";C;" LAUGHS."
```

T/S   On the Timex Sinclair you must start by setting C at zero, like this:

```
5 LET C=Ø
```

When you run that program, you should see

```
Ø
HI
1
HO
2
HA
3
HEE HEE
4
THAT MAKES 4 LAUGHS.
```

Do you see how the counter $C = C + 1$ kept track of the number of times you printed something?

Usually you'll find a counter like that in a subroutine. Every time the computer goes to the subroutine it adds one to keep track of the score. For example, to write that program with a subroutine, you would do this:

```
10 PRINT C
20 PRINT "HI"
30 GOSUB 1000
40 PRINT "HO"
50 GOSUB 1000
60 PRINT "HA"
70 GOSUB 1000
80 PRINT "HEE HEE"
90 GOSUB 1000
100 PRINT "THAT MAKES ";C;" LAUGHS."
990 END
1000 C=C+1
1005 PRINT C
1010 RETURN
```

13. Score Your Quizzes.

Here's a more useful example of a counter in a program: keeping track of right and wrong answers when you're answering questions. This is a silly quiz program. Maybe you'd like to use this example to write a more serious one.

```
NEW
10 (clear the screen)
20 PRINT "WHAT GOES MEOW?"
30 A$="CAT"
40 GOSUB 1000
50 PRINT "HOW MANY LEGS DOES A DUCK HAVE?"
60 A$="2"
70 GOSUB 1000
80 PRINT "WHAT WAS MRS. WASHINGTON'S FIRST NAME?"
90 A$="MARTHA"
```

```
1ØØ GOSUB 1ØØØ
11Ø PRINT "WHO WENT UP THE HILL WITH JACK?"
12Ø A$="JILL"
13Ø GOSUB 1ØØØ
9ØØ PRINT "THAT'S ALL!"
91Ø PRINT "YOU GOT ";R;" RIGHT OUT OF ";Q
92Ø PRINT "YOU MISSED ";W;" OUT OF ";Q
99Ø END
1ØØØ REM ADDS TOTAL QUESTIONS, CHECKS ANSWER, AND KEEPS
SCORE
1Ø1Ø INPUT B$
1Ø2Ø Q=Q+1
1Ø3Ø IF A$=B$ THEN R=R+1:PRINT "RIGHT!"
1Ø4Ø IF A$<>B$ THEN W=W+1: PRINT "NO THE ANSWER IS ";A$
1Ø5Ø PRINT:PRINT "PLEASE PRESS RETURN"
1Ø6Ø INPUT R$
1Ø7Ø (clear the screen)
1Ø8Ø RETURN
```

ᴧ   Remember, for the Atari add: 1 DIM A$(2Ø),B$(2Ø),R$(1)

TI T/S On the TI and Timex Sinclair you must rewrite the IF . . . THEN routines, as explained in Chapter 7.

Notice, in the subroutine, that the program uses Q to keep track of the total number of questions. It gets to that line with the GOSUB 1ØØØ that follows every answer. So each time through one question it adds 1 to the total for Q. Since the program does line 1030 only if the answer is correct, it uses R in that line to keep track of the number of right answers. In line 1040 it uses W to keep track of the number of wrong answers. Then at the end it prints the total score.

Here's a sample run of that program:

```
WHAT GOES MEOW?
? CAT
RIGHT!
PLEASE PRESS RETURN
```

HOW MANY LEGS DOES A DUCK HAVE?

? *2*

RIGHT!

PLEASE PRESS RETURN

WHAT WAS MRS. WASHINGTON'S FIRST NAME?

? *SARAH*

NO, THE ANSWER IS MARTHA

PLEASE PRESS RETURN

WHO WENT UP THE HILL WITH JACK?

? *JILL*

RIGHT!

PLEASE PRESS RETURN

THAT'S ALL!

YOU GOT 3 RIGHT OUT OF 4.

YOU MISSED 1 OUT OF 4.

Practice 10

1. Write a program in which the computer asks you your name and then prints it 10 times.
2. Add a timing delay loop to the program in question 1 so the computer pauses after each time it prints your name.
3. Write a program to make the computer print the 3 times table, from 3×0 to 3×12. (Can you do this two different ways — with and without the **STEP** command?)
4. Use the program in Section 8 of Chapter 8 (headed **GOSUB YES** or **GOSUB NO**). Try adding a counter to the **YES** subroutine to keep track of right answers and one to the **NO** subroutine to keep track of wrong answers. Then add 2 lines at the end of the program to print how many you got right and how many you missed.

Answers to Practice 10

1.
```
1Ø PRINT "WHAT'S YOUR NAME?"
2Ø INPUT N$
3Ø FOR X=1 TO 1Ø
4Ø PRINT N$
5Ø NEXT X
```
🔺 On the Atari, don't forget to add **DIM N$**.

2.   `45 FOR T=1 TO 3ØØ:NEXT T`

Note: The number 300 in that line may be changed to vary the speed.

3.

Method 1:
```
1Ø FOR X=Ø TO 36 STEP 3
2Ø PRINT X
3Ø NEXT X
```
Method 2:
```
1Ø FOR X=Ø TO 12
2Ø PRINT X*3
3Ø NEXT X
```

4. Add these lines, or similar ones, to that program:
```
2Ø75 R=R+1
3Ø75 W=W+1

991 PRINT "YOU GOT ";R;"RIGHT."
992 PRINT "YOU GOT ";W;"WRONG."
```

11.
DATA: It's What Your Computer Loves to READ

DATA and READ are two words that always go together in BASIC programs.

DATA means "Here is a list of things."

READ means "Go find each item on the list, in order."

T/S *Note:* If you have a Timex Sinclair computer, skip this chapter. The version of BASIC on the Timex Sinclair 1000 does not include DATA.

1. Reading Numbers.

Type this program:

```
NEW
1Ø DATA 2,4,6
2Ø READ A
3Ø PRINT A
```

When you run that program, the computer prints 2. Here's why:

Line 10 means "Here is a list: 2, 4, 6"

Line 20 means "Go find the first number on the list and let A stand for that number."

Line 30 means "Print the number that equals A."

The letter **A** in that program, as you should know by now, is a *variable*. So far our programs have used variables as **INPUT**, as random numbers (with **RND**), and for counting (as with **FOR . . . NEXT**). Now we're going to use variables as pieces of **DATA**.

When your program said **INPUT A**, it meant that the person running the program would tell the computer what **A** equals. When your program says **READ A**, it tells the computer to go and find what **A** equals in a **DATA** line.

The first time the computer sees the instruction **READ A**, it will take the first item on the list to equal **A**. In this program, the first item on the list was 2. So when you told the computer to **PRINT A**, the computer printed 2.

2. A Second Reading.

Now list the program and add these lines

        4Ø READ A
        5Ø PRINT A
        RUN

and the computer should print

        2
        4

In line 40 the computer found the instruction **READ A** for the second time in the program. That made it go and find the second item on the list. Since the second item was 4, the computer now has made **A** equal 4. (Remember that a variable means something that can change. The variable **A** will change to a different number every time the computer sees the instruction **READ A**.)

Let's tell the computer to **READ** and **PRINT A** once again. This time we'll put both statements in one line of the program, like this:

        6Ø READ A : PRINT A

TI   *Remember:* If you have a TI computer, you may not use a colon. You will have to make two lines like this:

        6Ø READ A
        65 PRINT A

What should the computer print now when you run the program? Try it and see if you were right.

3. The End of the Line.

We have three numbers in our **DATA** line, and we've told the computer to **READ** three times. What will happen if we tell it to **READ** one more time? Let's find out. Add this line:

        7Ø READ A

Run the program, and you will see that when the computer gets to Line 70 it is **OUT OF DATA**, and it will tell you so with an error message. In other words, the computer is saying, "You told me to keep on reading, but I've run out of things to read."

4. Streamline Your Reading.

We've put more lines in this program than we really needed so we could explain how the **READ** and **DATA** statements work. Here's a shorter way to make a program do the same thing. (Let's change the variable letter just to remind you that you can use any letter you want to.)

        NEW
        1Ø DATA 2,4,6
        2Ø READ N
        3Ø PRINT N
        4Ø GOTO 2Ø
        RUN

This will do exactly the same thing as the program just before it: make the computer print everything in the **DATA** line until it runs out of **DATA**. The **GOTO** statement makes the computer do line 20 over and over until there's nothing left to **READ**.

But of course, you don't really want to have that **OUT OF DATA ERROR** line cluttering up the screen after the computer finishes printing its whole list of data. So let's tell the computer what to do when it comes to the end of the list. Obviously, there are two things you can do when you come to the end of something you are reading. Either you can stop, or you can start over again. But the computer doesn't know which one to do unless you tell it. Let's first tell it to stop reading when it comes to the end. Add this line:

>   35 IF N = 6 THEN END

TI   But remember if you have a TI, you must follow **THEN** by a line number. So you will have to add two new lines:

>   35 IF N = 6 THEN 5Ø
>   5Ø END

If you are using a TI, you will also have to modify the other programs in this chapter by putting the **END** command in a separate line.

Line 35 tells the computer to end the program when it comes to 6, the last item on the list. Now run the program, and you'll see that the computer knows when to quit.

5. Starting Over Again.

Remember we said there were two things you could do when you finished what you were reading. We've told the computer how to stop reading. Now let's tell it how to start over again from the beginning. First list the program and look at the instructions again. It should look like this:

>   1Ø DATA 2,4,6
>   2Ø READ N
>   3Ø PRINT N
>   35 IF N = 6 THEN END
>   4Ø GOTO 2Ø

Now change line 35 to this:

>   35 IF N = 6 THEN RESTORE

TI   On the TI, leave line 35 as it was, change line 50, and add line 60:

>   5Ø RESTORE
>   6Ø GOTO 2Ø

RESTORE means "Start over again at the beginning of the **DATA**." So when you run this program now, it will just keep printing the list over and over again. This puts the computer in an endless loop, which you will have to stop by pressing the appropriate key. (Look back to Chapter 2 if you've forgotten it.)

6. String Up Some Words for Data.

Now let's make the computer use the **DATA** statement to print a list of words. (Remember how you tell the computer to expect a word for a variable — with the string sign, **$**.)

Note: Whenever you type a **DATA** line of words, be very careful not to put in any extra spaces before or after the commas. A space may confuse the computer into thinking that the space has to be part of the **DATA**.

```
NEW
1Ø PRINT "THESE ARE SOME OF MY FAVORITE PEOPLE."
2Ø DATA BEN,MARY,MIKE,SALLY
3Ø READ A$
4Ø PRINT A$
5Ø IF A$ = "SALLY" THEN END
6Ø GOTO 2Ø
```

⅄   On the Atari, add: 1 DIM A$(2Ø)

Run this program, then look at the listing to make sure you understand how it works. Then change line 20 to make the computer print a list of *your* favorite people.

Did you notice that when you change line 20, you will also have to change line 50? Since your list probably doesn't end with "Sally," you will have to tell the computer what is the last name on your list. For that reason, programmers usually make the last item on a data list the word **END**. So a better way to write that program would be like this:

```
1Ø PRINT "THESE ARE SOME OF MY FAVORITE PEOPLE."
2Ø DATA BEN,MARY,MIKE,SALLY
```

```
25 DATA END
30 READ A$
35 IF A$="END" THEN END
40 PRINT A$
60 GOTO 20
```

Do you understand why we had to move the **IF . . . THEN** line from 50 to 35? If we left the **PRINT** order first, the computer would think it was supposed to print **END**. So unless you have a friend whose name is **END**, you have to tell the computer to stop printing as soon as it **READ**s the word **END**.

With this program, you can type in your list of favorite people by changing only one line.

How would you change line 35 to make the computer print your list over and over again? If you've forgotten the word that means "start over," look back in Section 5 just above.

7. Reading Two Things At Once.

You can have your program read for more than one piece of **DATA** at a time like this:

```
NEW
10 DATA MARY,BOB,SALLY,PETER,PAM,FRANK,END,END
20 READ G$,B$
30 IF B$="END" THEN END
40 PRINT G$;" LOVES ";B$
50 GOTO 20
```

⚛   On the Atari, add: 1 DIM G$(20),B$(20)

In this program **G$** stands for the first item on the **DATA** list, and **B$** stands for the second item. The second time the computer reads the list, **G$** will be the third item and **B$** the fourth item, etc., like this:

MARY,	BOB,	SALLY,	PETER,	PAM,	FRANK,	END,	END
G$	B$	G$	B$	G$	B$	G$	B$
1ST READ		2ND READ		3RD READ		4TH READ	

Notice that you must put END in the DATA line two times, so you have one END to stand for G\$ and one END to stand for B\$. If you put in only one END, the computer would run OUT OF DATA before it finished READing, because it wouldn't be able to match up *both* G\$ and B\$ the last time it went through the list.

You've probably figured out that we set up the DATA so that every G\$ would be a girl, and every B\$ would be a boy. Then the PRINT line can just plug in the right name from the DATA list and tell us which girl loves which boy.

If you haven't run this program yet, check it out now. You might want to change the DATA line to put in names of your friends.

8. DATA Meets INPUT.

Here's a slightly different version of that program, which lets you combine DATA with INPUT.

```
NEW
1Ø DATA MARY,BOB,SALLY,PETER,PAM,FRANK
15 DATA END,END
2Ø PRINT "NAME A GIRL."
3Ø INPUT N$
4Ø READ G$,B$
5Ø IF N$=G$ THEN PRINT G$;" LOVES ";B$
6Ø IF N$<>G$ THEN GOTO 4Ø
```

⋏   On the Atari, add: 1 DIM G\$(2Ø),B\$(2Ø),N\$(2Ø)

Run this program, but don't worry about any OUT OF DATA error. We'll fix that in a minute.

First, here's a description of how the program works so far:

Line 10: Gives the computer a list of girls' and boys' names.

Line 15: The end of the DATA. If you put the END statements in a separate line, it makes it easier to change the other DATA. You can have as many DATA lines in your program as you need to handle all your data. Just remember to start each line with the word DATA.

Line 20: Asks you (or whoever is running the program) to type in a girl's name.

Line 30: Waits for you to type the name, and uses **N$** to stand for the name you type in.

Line 40: Checks the list of **DATA**. The first time the computer reads the list, **G$** will stand for "MARY" and **B$** for "BOB." The second time **G$** will be "SALLY" and **B$** will be "PETER," and so forth.

Line 50: Checks to see if the girl's name you typed in (**N$**) is the same as the first girl's name on the list. In other words, does **N$** = **G$**, or in the first case, does **N$** = "MARY"? If it does, then print "MARY LOVES BOB."

Line 60: If **N$** does not equal **G$** (that is, if you did not type in "MARY"), then go back to line 40. That line will make the computer check the list again to see if it can find another **G$** to match with **N$**.

Now so far this program will only work correctly if you type in a name on its **DATA** list. Test this. Run the program and type in **PAT** or **SUE** or some other name not on the list when the computer asks you for a name. What message do you get?

So let's fix this program to make it work when you type a name that's not on its list. List the program and add lines 45 and 70 so that the whole program looks like this:

```
1Ø DATA MARY,BOB,SALLY,PETER,PAM,FRANK
15 DATA END,END
2Ø PRINT "NAME A GIRL."
3Ø INPUT N$
4Ø READ G$,B$
45 IF B$ = "END" THEN PRINT "SORRY, I DON'T KNOW    ";N$ : GOTO
7Ø
5Ø IF N$=G$ THEN PRINT G$;" LOVES ";B$
6Ø IF N$<>G$ THEN GOTO 4Ø
7Ø RESTORE : GOTO 2Ø
```

Line 45 tells the computer what to do when it comes to the end of the **DATA** list, so it doesn't send you an **OUT OF DATA** error message. Then it sends the computer down to line 70.

Line 70 tells the computer to start the program over again. **RESTORE**, you remember, means to go back to the beginning of the DATA list, and GOTO 2Ø will send the computer back to give you a chance to type in another girl's name.

Run the program (changing the DATA line if you like) and study the listing to make sure you understand how it works.

Notice that we have not made this program end. In order to stop it, you'll have to break into the loop at the INPUT line. Maybe you'd like to figure out how to add some lines to give you a way out of the program.

Hint: After you RESTORE the data in line 70, don't go back to line 20. Instead make line 70 ask you whether you want to type another name. Then write your program to allow you that choice. You will need a PRINT statement for the question, an INPUT line for the answer, and an IF . . . THEN statement that starts the program over if you answer yes. If you don't answer yes, the program ends. (If you get stuck, check the solution in the answer section for this chapter.)

9. A Loverly Quiz.

By changing part of this program, it becomes a quiz:

```
NEW
1Ø DATA MARY,BOB,SALLY,PETER,PAM,FRANK
15 DATA END,END
2Ø READ G$,B$
3Ø IF B$="END" THEN END
4Ø PRINT "WHO DOES ";G$;" LOVE?"
5Ø INPUT L$
6Ø IF L$=B$ THEN PRINT "YES!"
7Ø IF L$<>B$ THEN PRINT "NO, ";G$;" LOVES ";B$
8Ø GOTO 2Ø
```

⅄   Atari, add: 1 DIM G$(2Ø),B$(2Ø),L$(2Ø)

Type in this program and run it, then look at the line by line explanation below:

Line 10: Makes a list of girls' and boys' names.

Line 15: End statement.

Line 20: Makes the computer READ the first two names on the DATA list. The first time around, G$ will be "MARY" and B$ will be "BOB".

Line 30: Tells the computer to end the program when it gets to the end of the DATA lines.

Line 40: The computer asks the question: "Who does Mary (the first G$) love?"

Line 50: Waits for you to type in the name of Mary's boyfriend.

Line 60: Checks to see if L$ (the name you typed in) is the same as B$ (or Bob). If you did type in "BOB", the computer prints "YES!"

Line 70: If you did not type in "BOB", the computer tells you that you're wrong, Mary loves Bob.

Line 80: Sends you back to line 20, to READ the next two names on the DATA list, and go through the program again.

10. Computers and Capitals: Two More Quizzes.

Here are two more examples of quizzes you can write using DATA . . . READ. Since one piece of data can be more than one word, you can make your data statements include whole questions. When the computer is READing the DATA, it takes everything between commas to be one string variable.

```
NEW
1Ø DATA WHAT LANGUAGE IS THIS COMPUTER USING?,BASIC
2Ø DATA WHAT WORD MAKES THE COMPUTER START DOING A PRO-
GRAM?,RUN
3Ø DATA WHAT WORD SHOULD YOU TYPE BEFORE YOU BEGIN WRITING
A PROGRAM?,NEW
4Ø DATA END,END
5Ø READ Q$,A$
6Ø IF A$="END" THEN END
7Ø PRINT Q$
8Ø INPUT B$
9Ø IF B$=A$ THEN PRINT "RIGHT!"
```

```
100 IF B$<>A$ THEN PRINT "NO, IT'S ";A$
110 GOTO 50
```

⼈   Atari, add: 1 DIM Q$(100),A$(20),B$(20)

You can see how easy it becomes to write a quiz program with **DATA** statements. Just use this model, and put in any questions you want.

Note: If you want to have a comma inside one piece of **DATA**, then put the whole piece of **DATA** inside quotes, like this:

```
25 DATA "IN BASIC Z, X, N, A$, AND Q$ ARE EXAMPLES OF WHAT?",
VARIABLES
```

Another example of a program that might help you study is this one, which tests you on states and capitals:

```
NEW
10 DATA MASSACHUSETTS,BOSTON,NEW YORK,ALBANY,
CALIFORNIA,SACRAMENTO
20 DATA TEXAS,AUSTIN,NEBRASKA,LINCOLN,NEW MEXICO,SANTA FE
30 DATA END,END
40 READ S$,C$
50 IF C$="END" THEN END
60 PRINT "WHAT IS THE CAPITAL OF ";S$
70 INPUT A$
80 IF A$=C$ THEN PRINT "RIGHT!"
90 IF A$<>C$ THEN PRINT "NO, IT'S ";C$
100 GOTO 40
```

⼈   Atari, add: 1 DIM A$(20),S$(20),C$(20)

Of course, you can add more **DATA** lines to make the program include the capitals of all 50 states in the U.S.

11. The Computer's a Poet but Doesn't Know It.

You'll find **READ** . . . **DATA** is one of the most useful statements when writing **BASIC** programs. It lets you make all kinds of shortcuts and change programs very easily by retyping only a few lines.

Here's an example of how to use **DATA** lines to help you write a poem. Suppose you're trying to think of a word to rhyme with "boat." First think of all the initial consonants and blends that you can, and put them in **DATA** lines. Write your program so you can put the sound you want to rhyme in an **INPUT** line. Then let the computer put the words together for you. You'll come up with a lot of nonsense words, but you'll probably also get some real words you never thought of.

Here's the program:

```
NEW
1Ø DATA B,C,D,F,G,H,J,K,L,M,N,P,QU,R,S,T,V,W,Y,Z
2Ø DATA BR,BL,CH,CR,CL,FL,FR,GR,GL,PR,PH,PL
3Ø DATA ST,SH,SP,SCR,STR,TH,TR,THR
4Ø DATA END
5Ø PRINT "TYPE THE RHYMING SOUND"
6Ø INPUT S$
7Ø READ B$
8Ø IF B$="END" THEN END
1ØØ PRINT B$;S$;" ";
11Ø GOTO 7Ø
```

Ⱥ   On the Atari begin with: 1 DIM S$(1Ø),B$(4)

Here's a sample run:

```
TYPE THE RHYMING SOUND
?OAT
BOAT COAT DOAT FOAT GOAT HOAT JOAT KOAT LOAT MOAT NOAT POAT
QUOAT ROAT SOAT TOAT VOAT WOAT YOAT ZOAT BROAT BLOAT CHOAT
CROAT CLOAT FLOAT FROAT GROAT GLOAT PROAT PHOAT PLOAT
STOAT SHOAT SPOAT SCROAT STROAT THOAT TROAT THROAT
```

You can, of course, add to that program by putting more blends in the data line. Also you can run through it again with -OTE for your ending sound and get more rhyming words. (For example **NOTE** and **VOTE**.)

Practice 11

1. Write a program using **DATA** statements to make the computer print a list of animals.

2. Write a program using **DATA** statements to make the computer print a list of animals and what they eat.

   Sample run:

   >DOGS EAT BONES
   >COWS EAT GRASS
   >BUNNIES EAT CARROTS
   >etc.

3. Change the program in Problem 2 to make it a quiz program.

   Sample run:

   >WHAT DO DOGS EAT?
   >?*CATS*
   >NO, DOGS EAT BONES
   >WHAT DO COWS EAT?
   >?*GRASS*
   >RIGHT!
   >WHAT DO BUNNIES EAT?
   >?*CARROTS*
   >RIGHT!
   >etc.

Answers to Practice 11:

1.
```
1Ø DATA DOGS,COWS,BUNNIES,CATS,ELEPHANTS,MICE
2Ø DATA END
3Ø READ A$
4Ø IF A$="END" THEN END
```

```
            5Ø PRINT A$
            6Ø GOTO 3Ø
2.          1Ø DATA DOGS,BONES,COWS,GRASS,BUNNIES,CARROTS
            2Ø DATA END,END
            3Ø READ A$,B$
            4Ø IF A$="END" THEN END
            5Ø PRINT A$;" EAT ";B$
```

3. Lines 10–40 will be the same as above. Here is the rest of the program:

```
            5Ø PRINT "WHAT DO ";A$;" EAT?"
            6Ø INPUT C$
            7Ø IF C$=B$ THEN PRINT "RIGHT":GOTO 3Ø
            8Ø PRINT "NO, ";A$;" EAT ";B$:GOTO 3Ø
```

     ᴧ   (On all programs on the Atari, don't forget to DIMension your strings.)

12.
Putting It All Together

This chapter will present just a few sample programs, showing how some people have had fun thinking up ideas for ways to use their computers. If you want to try any of these programs, go ahead and type them in. But the main purpose of this chapter is to give you some ideas to keep going on your own. Think about ways you can use your computer — just for fun, to entertain your friends, to help you with problems, or to make your life a little easier in some way. Then either try to write your own program or look for one that's already been written and think about whether you could make it better for you. Have fun!

Note: These programs will work on the Apple, Atari, Commodore, or TRS-80 computers. They will have to be rewritten for the TI to avoid more than one BASIC statement in a line. Programs with DATA statements will not work on the Timex Sinclair 1000.

1. A Little Brain-Teasing.

This is a quiz program just for fun — to prove that things aren't always the way they seem.

```
NEW
Ø REM GAME WRITTEN BY BEN AULT
5 (clear the screen)
1Ø PRINT "THIS GAME IS CALLED QWERT"
2Ø PRINT:PRINT "WHAT IS YOUR NAME?"
3Ø INPUT A$
4Ø PRINT:PRINT "OH TOUGH LUCK, ";A$
45 PRINT
5Ø PRINT "I WILL NOW ASK YOU SOME QUESTIONS."
55 GOSUB 1ØØØ
6Ø PRINT "IF A ROOSTER SITS ON TOP OF A BARN WITH A SLANTING
ROOF"
7Ø PRINT "WILL THE EGG ROLL OFF THE ROOF?"
8Ø INPUT S$
9Ø IF S$="YES" THEN PRINT "WRONG!"
1ØØ IF S$="NO" THEN PRINT "CORRECT!"
11Ø PRINT "ROOSTERS DON'T LAY EGGS."
12Ø GOSUB 1ØØØ
13Ø PRINT "IF YOU TAKE 2 APPLES FROM 3 APPLES, HOW MANY APPLES
DO YOU HAVE?"
14Ø PRINT "TYPE THE NUMBER."
15Ø INPUT E
16Ø IF E=2 THEN PRINT "CORRECT":GOTO 18Ø
17Ø PRINT "WRONG"
18Ø PRINT "IF YOU TAKE 2 APPLES YOU HAVE 2 APPLES."
19Ø GOSUB 1ØØØ
2ØØ PRINT "IS IT POSSIBLE FOR JANE TO STAND BEHIND LEE"
21Ø PRINT "AND LEE TO STAND BEHIND JANE AT THE SAME TIME?"
22Ø INPUT W$
23Ø IF W$="YES" THEN PRINT "ABSOLUTELY!"
24Ø IF W$="NO" THEN PRINT "INCORRECT"
25Ø PRINT "THEY CAN STAND BACK TO BACK."
```

```
260 GOSUB 1000
270 PRINT "HOW MANY 3-CENT STAMPS IN A DOZEN?"
280 INPUT U
290 IF U=12 THEN PRINT "CORRECT":GOTO 310
300 PRINT "FOOLED YOU!"
310 PRINT "THERE ARE ALWAYS 12 IN A DOZEN."
320 GOSUB 1000
330 PRINT "A BOTTLE AND A CAP TOGETHER COST $1.10."
340 PRINT "THE BOTTLE COSTS ONE DOLLAR MORE THAN THE CAP."
350 PRINT "HOW MUCH DOES THE CAP COST?"
355 PRINT "TYPE THE NUMBER OF CENTS."
360 INPUT L
370 IF L=5 THEN PRINT "GOOD THINKING!":GOTO 390
380 PRINT "SORRY!"
390 PRINT "5 CENTS FOR THE BOTTLE AND $1.05 FOR THE CAP =
$1.10."
400 GOSUB 1000
410 PRINT "WHAT IS THE NAME OF THIS PROGRAM?"
420 INPUT K$
430 IF K$="QWERT" THEN PRINT "THANKS FOR
REMEMBERING.":GOTO 450
440 PRINT "WELL, I HAVE A BETTER MEMORY THAN YOU."
450 PRINT "I REMEMBER YOUR NAME, ";A$
460 PRINT "THANKS FOR PLAYING QWERT, ";A$
470 PRINT:PRINT "ADIOS, AU REVOIR, ARRIVIDERCI,"
480 PRINT "SAYONARA, AUF WIEDERSEHN,"
490 PRINT "AND GOOD-BYE!"
500 END
1000 PRINT:PRINT "PLEASE PRESS RETURN"
1010 INPUT R$
1020 (clear the screen)
1030 RETURN
```

Ⱥ   On the Atari, remember to DIMension your strings:
2 DIM A$(2Ø),S$(5),W$(5),K$(1Ø),R$(1)

TRS   On the TRS-80 in line 1000 you would say "PLEASE PRESS ENTER."
(You will also have to substitute ENTER for RETURN in similar lines in
the other programs in this chapter.)

Here's a sample run (omitting the lines that say "Please press return" to clear
the screen after each question).

THIS GAME IS CALLED QWERT.
WHAT IS YOUR NAME?
? *MIKE*
OH, TOUGH LUCK, MIKE

I WILL NOW ASK YOU SOME QUESTIONS.
IF A ROOSTER SITS ON TOP OF A BARN WITH A SLANTING ROOF WILL
THE EGG ROLL OFF THE ROOF?
? *YES*
WRONG!
ROOSTERS DON'T LAY EGGS.

IF YOU TAKE 2 APPLES FROM 3 APPLES, HOW MANY APPLES DO YOU
HAVE?
TYPE THE NUMBER.
? *1*
WRONG!
IF YOU TAKE 2 APPLES YOU HAVE 2 APPLES.

IS IT POSSIBLE FOR JANE TO STAND BEHIND LEE
AND LEE TO STAND BEHIND JANE AT THE SAME TIME?
? *YES*
ABSOLUTELY!
THEY CAN STAND BACK TO BACK.

HOW MANY 3-CENT STAMPS IN A DOZEN?
? *4*

FOOLED YOU!
THERE ARE ALWAYS 12 IN A DOZEN.

A BOTTLE AND A CAP TOGETHER COST $1.10.
THE BOTTLE COSTS ONE DOLLAR MORE THAN THE CAP.
HOW MUCH DOES THE CAP COST?
TYPE THE NUMBER OF CENTS.
? *10*
SORRY!
5 CENTS FOR THE BOTTLE AND $1.05 FOR THE CAP = $1.10.

WHAT IS THE NAME OF THIS PROGRAM?
? *QUERT*
WELL, I HAVE A BETTER MEMORY THAN YOU.
I REMEMBER YOUR NAME, MIKE.

THANKS FOR PLAYING QWERT, MIKE.
ADIOS, AU REVOIR, ARRIVIDERCI,
SAYONARA, AUF WIEDERSEHN,
AND GOOD-BYE!

2. Spelling Practice.

Here's a program to help you practice your spelling. Use line 10 (and as many other lines as you need from 11 to 19) to type in your spelling words as DATA.

When you run the program, it flashes the words quickly on the screen and asks you to type in the correct spelling. When you misspell a word, the program goes to line 140, where it keeps count of the mistakes (with W) and begins a routine that makes it print the correct spelling 9 times so you can study it. Then it goes back to give you another chance.

Some teachers have used this program in their classrooms, with this addition: A game (copied from a computer book or magazine, or made up by students) is added to the end of the program. If the student gets all the words right (IF W=Ø), he or she gets to play the game. If not, the program ends.

```
NEW
Ø REM THANKS TO S. NOCELLA AND C. KWARCINSKI
5 (clear the screen)
1Ø DATA CAT,DOG,BOY,GIRL
2Ø DATA END
3Ø PRINT "SPELLING QUIZ"
4Ø PRINT:PRINT "PLEASE PRESS RETURN AND WATCH CAREFULLY FOR
THE WORD."
5Ø INPUT R$
6Ø (clear the screen)
7Ø READ W$
75 IF W$="END" THEN PRINT "THAT'S ALL THE WORDS FOR
TODAY":GOTO 25Ø
8Ø PRINT W$
85 REM ADJUST NUMBER IN LINE 9Ø FOR LONGER OR SHORTER FLASH
9Ø FOR T=1 TO 2ØØ:NEXT T
1ØØ (clear the screen)
11Ø PRINT "TYPE THE WORD AND PRESS RETURN"
12Ø INPUT A$
13Ø IF A$=W$ THEN PRINT "GOOD SPELLING!":PRINT:PRINT "PLEASE
PRESS RETURN FOR THE NEXT WORD.":GOTO 5Ø
135 REM LINES 14Ø-23Ø ALLOW STUDENT TO REVIEW SPELLING OF
MISSED WORDS
14Ø W=W+1
145 PRINT:PRINT "NO, WATCH CAREFULLY."
146 PRINT
15Ø FOR X=1 TO 3
16Ø FOR T=1 TO 1ØØ:NEXT T
17Ø FOR Y=1 TO 3: PRINT W$;" ";
175 FOR T=1 TO 1ØØ:NEXT T
```

```
180 NEXT Y
185 PRINT
190 NEXT X
195 FOR Z = 1 TO 2000: NEXT Z
200 PRINT:PRINT "PLEASE PRESS RETURN AND TRY AGAIN."
210 INPUT R$
220 (clear the screen)
230 GOTO 80
250 IF W=0 THEN PRINT "YOU GOT 100% RIGHT!":END
260 PRINT "YOU MISSED ";W
```

⅄   On the Atari, add 1 DIM A$(20),W$(20)

Here's a sample run of the program:

```
SPELLING QUIZ
PLEASE PRESS RETURN AND WATCH CAREFULLY FOR THE WORD.
CAT
```

(*Note:* The word flashes on, then disappears.)

```
TYPE THE WORD AND PRESS RETURN
? KAT
NO, WATCH CAREFULLY.
CAT CAT CAT
CAT CAT CAT
CAT CAT CAT
PLEASE PRESS RETURN AND TRY AGAIN.
CAT
TYPE THE WORD AND PRESS RETURN
? CAT
GOOD SPELLING!
PLEASE PRESS RETURN FOR THE NEXT WORD.
DOG
TYPE THE WORD AND PRESS RETURN
? DOG
GOOD SPELLING!
```

PLEASE PRESS RETURN FOR THE NEXT WORD.
BOY
TYPE THE WORD AND PRESS RETURN.
? *BOY*
GOOD SPELLING!
PLEASE PRESS RETURN FOR THE NEXT WORD.
GIRL
TYPE THE WORD AND PRESS RETURN.
? *GIRL*
GOOD SPELLING!
PLEASE PRESS RETURN FOR THE NEXT WORD.
THAT'S ALL THE WORDS FOR TODAY!
YOU MISSED 1

3. Math Dice.

Here's a game that could help you practice math facts. This version uses addition, but it could easily be changed to subtraction or multiplication. In this version, we've pretended to be using regular dice, so the numbers only go up to 6. If you want to use special dice and make your numbers bigger, change the range of random numbers.

This is a game for two players. Each one takes turns rolling two imaginary dice. (Actually the computer rolls the dice and prints the numbers.) If you can add the total on the two dice correctly, that total gets added to your score. You get two tries to answer correctly — and for each incorrect answer 5 points are deducted from your score. The computer keeps score, of course.

Here's the program:

```
NEW
Ø REM THANKS TO P. KEEFE AND E. WARWICK
1Ø (clear the screen)
2Ø PRINT "THIS IS A GAME FOR TWO PLAYERS."
3Ø PRINT "YOU WILL TAKE TURNS ROLLING DICE."
```

31 PRINT: PRINT "IF YOU CAN ADD THE TOTAL OF THE TWO DICE CORRECTLY,"

32 PRINT "THE COMPUTER WILL ADD THAT TOTAL TO YOUR SCORE."

33 PRINT:PRINT "YOU GET TWO TRIES TO ANSWER CORRECTLY."

34 PRINT "EACH WRONG ANSWER COSTS YOU 5 POINTS."

35 PRINT:PRINT "PLEASE PRESS RETURN TO START."

36 INPUT R$

37 (clear the screen)

4Ø PRINT "PLEASE TYPE THE NAME OF THE FIRST PLAYER."

5Ø INPUT F$

6Ø PRINT "THE SECOND PLAYER?"

7Ø INPUT S$

74 REM X AND Y KEEP TRACK OF WRONG ANSWERS—RESET TO Ø BEFORE EACH TURN

75 X=Ø:Y=Ø

76 (clear the screen)

8Ø PRINT F$;" IS ROLLING THE DICE."

9Ø R=INT(RND(1)*6)+1

1ØØ L=INT(RND(1)*6)+1

TRS $\begin{cases} \\ \\ \end{cases}$ 9Ø RANDOM:R=RND(6)

1ØØ L=RND(6)

11Ø PRINT "THE RIGHT ONE SAYS ";R

12Ø PRINT "THE LEFT ONE SAYS ";L

13Ø PRINT "WHAT IS THE TOTAL?"

14Ø INPUT A

15Ø IF A=R+L THEN F=F+R+L:PRINT "RIGHT!":PRINT "YOUR SCORE IS ";F:GOTO 19Ø

159 REM ROUTINE FOR WRONG ANSWER

16Ø X=X+1

17Ø IF X<2 THEN PRINT "NO, TRY AGAIN.":F=F−5:GOTO 14Ø

18Ø PRINT "NO THE ANSWER IS ";R+L

```
190 PRINT
200 PRINT S$;"'S TURN"
210 I=INT(RND(1)*6)+1
220 E=INT(RND(1)*6)+1
```

TRS⎰
```
210 RANDOM:I=RND(6)
220 E=RND(6)
```

```
230 PRINT "ONE DIE SAYS ";I
240 PRINT "THE OTHER SAYS ";E
250 PRINT "WHAT IS THE TOTAL?"
260 INPUT B
270 IF B=I+E THEN S=S+I+E:PRINT "RIGHT!":GOTO 305
280 Y=Y+1
290 IF Y<2 THEN PRINT "NO, TRY AGAIN.":S=S-5:GOTO 260
300 PRINT "NO, THE ANSWER IS ";I+E
305 PRINT
310 PRINT S$;"'S SCORE IS ";S
315 PRINT
320 PRINT F$;"'S SCORE IS ";F
330 PRINT:PRINT "DO YOU WANT TO ROLL AGAIN?"
340 PRINT "TYPE Y FOR YES AND N FOR NO."
350 INPUT Y$
360 IF Y$="Y" THEN GOTO 75
370 IF Y$="N" THEN PRINT "OKAY. SEE YOU LATER.":END
380 PRINT "PLEASE TYPE Y OR N."
```

On the Atari remember to add line 1:

```
1 DIM F$(20),S$(20),Y$(3)
```

Here's part of a sample run of that program, beginning after the instructions.

```
MICKEY IS ROLLING THE DICE.
THE RIGHT ONE SAYS 5
THE LEFT ONE SAYS 5
WHAT IS THE TOTAL?
```

```
? 10
RIGHT! YOUR SCORE IS 1Ø
MINNIE'S TURN:
ONE DIE SAYS 1
THE OTHER SAYS 5
WHAT IS THE TOTAL?
? 6
RIGHT!
MINNIE'S SCORE IS 6
MICKEY'S SCORE IS 1Ø
DO YOU WANT TO ROLL AGAIN?
TYPE Y FOR YES AND N FOR NO. Y
MICKEY IS ROLLING THE DICE.
THE RIGHT ONE SAYS 6
THE LEFT ONE SAYS 6
WHAT IS THE TOTAL?
? 11
NO, TRY AGAIN.
? 12
RIGHT! YOUR SCORE IS 17
MINNIE'S TURN:
ONE DIE SAYS 4
THE OTHER SAYS 2
WHAT IS THE TOTAL?
? 6
RIGHT!
MINNIE'S SCORE IS 12
MICKEY'S SCORE IS 17
```
. . . and so on.

4. Politics.

In this program you must decide how you would deal with the problems that could arise if you were the mayor of a town. You start with $100,000. Your object is to spend your money in ways that will please the voters and get you re-elected, while staying within your budget. Here's an explanation of some parts of the program:

Lines 15–40 print the title and instructions.

Lines 45–320 involve many variables and random number routines to create the course of events in the game. Here's a description of some of the variables:

B — the amount of money in your budget.

T — how many times you've had a problem come up.

X — picks a random number for selecting a problem from the DATA list. (It is possible, as in real life, for the same problem to come up more than once in the game.)

P$ — the statement of the problem.

C — the cost of solving the problem.

A — adds or subtracts a random amount to or from the estimated cost, in order to establish the actual cost.

N — how many times you said no.

E — a random increase in the budget.

YV — your votes in the election. (The random formula for arriving at your votes subtracts something according to how many times you voted no on issues.)

DV — the dogcatcher's votes.

Lines 325–660 are some possible outcomes for the game — based on a combination of random factors and how you decided to spend your money.

Lines 700–750 are 22 possible problems, and their estimated cost. You could, of course, add to or change these. If you add more problems, you will have to change the range in line 60, which is set for 22 problems. For example, if you add five more problems, change that number to 27.

Note. If you have a TRS-80, look for the starred (***) lines and substitute the lines at the end of the program.

```
NEW
1Ø (clear the screen)
15 PRINT ">POLITICS"
```

```
20 PRINT " (C) 1982 BY MIKE AULT":PRINT
25 PRINT "IN THIS GAME YOU ARE THE MAYOR OF A SMALL TOWN."
30 PRINT:PRINT "YOU MUST DECIDE HOW TO SPEND YOUR
   BUDGET"
35 PRINT "TO DEAL WITH THE PROBLEMS THAT COME UP."
40 PRINT "YOUR OBJECT IS TO PLEASE THE VOTERS SO YOU CAN BE
   RE-ELECTED."
45 B = 100000:T=0:N=0
46 PRINT:PRINT "YOU START WITH $";B;"IN YOUR BUDGET."
***50 PRINT:PRINT "HIT RETURN. . .";:INPUT K$
55 (clear the screen): PRINT "BUDGET: $";B: IF B<0 THEN GOTO 500
57 T = T+ 1 :IF T > 10 THEN 300
***60 X = INT(RND(1) * 22) + 1: RESTORE
65 FOR I = 1 TO X: READ P$,C: NEXT I
70 PRINT:PRINT P$:PRINT:PRINT "ESTIMATED COST: $";C
75 PRINT:PRINT "DO YOU WANT TO SPEND THE MONEY (Y/N)";
76 INPUT K$
77 IF K$="Y" THEN 100
***80 N = N + 1: IF N > RND(1) * 6 + 4 THEN 400
***90 IF RND(1) > .92 THEN GOSUB 200
95 GOTO 50
***100 A=INT(RND(1) * (C/10)):IF RND(1) > .8 THEN A = −A
105 C = C + A: PRINT "ACTUAL COST: $";C : B = B − C
***110 IF RND(1) > .49 THEN GOSUB 200
115 GOTO 50
200 PRINT "VOTERS ELECT TO INCREASE YOUR BUDGET!!!"
***205 E = INT(RND(1) * 1000) + 500 : B = B + E
210 RETURN
300 (clear the screen)
310 PRINT "ELECTIONS!":PRINT "IT'S YOU AGAINST THE OLD
   DOGCATCHER!"
```

```
***315 PRINT:PRINT "VOTES: ": YV = INT(RND(1) * 1000 + 500) + 15 *
     (20-N): DV = 2000 - YV
   320 PRINT:PRINT "FOR YOU: ";YV: PRINT "FOR DOGCATCHER: ";DV
   325 PRINT: IF DV < YV THEN PRINT "YOU WON!!! NICE GOING, I
     KNEW YOU COULD DO IT!":GOTO 600
   330 IF DV = YV THEN 300
   335 PRINT "WELL, IT LOOKS LIKE YOU LOST."
   336 PRINT "BETTER LUCK NEXT TIME": GOTO 600
   400 (clear the screen)
   410 PRINT "VOTERS UNANIMOUSLY DECIDE TO KICK YOU OUT OF
     OFFICE!"
   415 PRINT "YOU'RE IN TROUBLE!"
   420 FOR I = 1 TO 1000: NEXT I
***425 IF RND(1) < .5 THEN GOTO 650
   430 PRINT "THE VOTERS MAY NOT LIKE YOU AS A MAYOR,"
   435 PRINT "BUT THEY FIND YOU A NEW JOB."
   440 PRINT "EVERYONE THINKS YOU'RE A TERRIFIC DOGCATCHER!":
     GOTO 600
   500 PRINT "THERE'S NO MONEY LEFT."
   510 PRINT "THE VOTERS KICK YOU OUT AND ELECT THE TOWN
     DOGCATCHER MAYOR."
   520 PRINT "YOU REALLY SCREWED UP THIS TIME!": GOTO 605
   600 PRINT:PRINT "YOU HAD $";B;" LEFT."
   605 PRINT:PRINT "PLAY AGAIN (Y/N)";
   610 INPUT K$
   615 IF K$="Y" THEN (clear the screen): GOTO 45
   620 PRINT "THANKS FOR PLAYING.": END
   650 PRINT "LUCKILY YOU MANAGED TO GRAB WHAT WAS LEFT IN
     THE BUDGET"
   655 PRINT "AND ESCAPE TO SUNNY BERMUDA."
   660 GOTO 600
   700 DATA THE LITTLE LEAGUE TEAM NEEDS NEW UNIFORMS.,500
   705 DATA A FLOOD HITS TOWN!! DAMAGE TO STREETS.,20000
```

71Ø DATA THE FIRE HOUSE JUST BURNED DOWN! WE NEED A NEW ONE.,3ØØØØ

715 DATA A TRUCK CRASHED INTO TOWN HALL! REPAIRS ARE NECESSARY.,5ØØØ

72Ø DATA THE TOWN COMPUTER BROKE DOWN—WE NEED TO HIRE A REPAIRMAN.,1ØØØ

725 DATA THE VOTERS WANT A STATUE PUT UP TO HONOR THE TOWN DOGCATCHER.,15ØØØ

73Ø DATA THE VOTERS DEMAND THAT YOU BUILD A TOWN PARK.,5ØØØØ

735 DATA THE TOWN DOGCATCHER NEEDS A NEW TRUCK AND MORE NETS.,1ØØØØ

74Ø DATA THE LIBRARY NEEDS TO REPLACE STOLEN BOOKS.,8ØØØ

745 DATA THE POLICE FORCE WANTS A NEW FLEET OF CRUISERS.,45ØØØ

75Ø DATA THE VOTERS DEMAND THAT YOU REPAIR THE POTHOLE-RIDDEN STREETS., 15ØØØ

755 DATA THE DOGCATCHER GOES ON STRIKE TO DEMAND MORE PAY.,5ØØØ

76Ø DATA THE VOTERS WANT THE TREES TRIMMED ON THE PUBLIC STREETS.,7ØØØ

765 DATA THE POLICE FORCE WANTS TO TRAIN NEW OFFICERS IN WATER BALLET.,1ØØØØ

77Ø DATA THE FIRE DEPARTMENT WANTS TO REPAINT THE HOOK AND LADDER TRUCKS.,15ØØ

775 DATA THE TOWN DUMP WANTS TO BUY A NEW TRASH COM-PACTOR UNIT., 2ØØØØ

78Ø DATA THE ROADS IN FRONT OF TOWN HALL NEED REPAVING.,1ØØØØ

785 DATA THE STREET LAMPS ALL NEED NEW BULBS.,9ØØØ

79Ø DATA THE TOWN WANTS NEW STREET SIGNS PUT UP AT EVERY CORNER.,15ØØØ

795 DATA TOWN OVERRUN WITH PESKY PETUNIAS! VOTERS

```
                    DEMAND YOU DESTROY THEM.,35ØØØ
                 8ØØ DATA THE DOGCATCHER WANTS A VACATION IN HAWAII.,5ØØØ
                 8Ø5 DATA STUDENTS LEAD PROTEST TO DEMAND BETTER FOOD IN
                    SCHOOL CAFETERIA.,1ØØØØ
```

⅃   On the Atari, add: 1 DIM P$(1ØØ),K$(5)

TRS   ***For the TRS-80 add this line: 1 CLEAR 1ØØ

Then change these lines as follows:

```
        5Ø PRINT:PRINT "HIT ENTER. . .";:INPUT K$
        6Ø RANDOM: X = RND(22): RESTORE
        8Ø N = N + 1:IF N>RND(6) + 4 THEN 4ØØ
        9Ø IF RND(Ø) > .92 THEN GOSUB 2ØØ
        1ØØ A = RND(C/1Ø): IF RND(Ø) > .8 THEN A = −A
        11Ø IF RND(Ø) > .49 THEN GOSUB 2ØØ
        2Ø5 E = RND(1ØØØ) + 5ØØ : B = B + E
        315 PRINT:PRINT "VOTES: ":YV = RND(1ØØØ) + 5ØØ + 15 * (2Ø−N) : DV
        = 2ØØØ − YV
        425 IF RND(Ø) < .5 THEN GOTO 65Ø
```

Here's an abbreviated sample run:

```
        >POLITICS
          (C) 1982 BY MIKE AULT

        IN THIS GAME YOU ARE THE MAYOR OF A SMALL TOWN.
        YOU MUST DECIDE  HOW TO SPEND YOUR BUDGET
        TO DEAL WITH THE PROBLEMS THAT COME UP.
        YOUR OBJECT IS TO PLEASE THE VOTERS SO YOU CAN BE RE-ELECTED.
        YOU START WITH $1ØØØØØ IN YOUR BUDGET.
        HIT RETURN. . .?

        BUDGET: $100000
        THE TOWN DUMP WANTS TO BUY A NEW TRASH COMPACTOR UNIT.
        ESTIMATED COST: $20000
        DO YOU WANT TO SPEND THE MONEY (Y/N)? N
        HIT RETURN. . .?
```

BUDGET: $100000

THE VOTERS DEMAND THAT YOU BUILD A TOWN PARK.

ESTIMATED COST: $50000

DO YOU WANT TO SPEND THE MONEY (Y/N)? *Y*

ACTUAL COST: $52453

VOTERS ELECT TO INCREASE YOUR BUDGET!!

HIT RETURN. . . ?

BUDGET: $48653

THE POLICE FORCE WANTS TO TRAIN NEW OFFICERS IN WATER BALLET.

ESTIMATED COST: $10000

DO YOU WANT TO SPEND THE MONEY (Y/N)? *N*

BUDGET: $48653

THE VOTERS WANT A STATUE PUT UP TO HONOR THE TOWN DOGCATCHER.

ESTIMATED COST: $15000

DO YOU WANT TO SPEND THE MONEY (Y/N)? *N*

BUDGET: $48653

THE FIRE DEPARTMENT WANTS TO REPAINT THE HOOK AND LADDER TRUCKS.

ESTIMATED COST: $1500

DO YOU WANT TO SPEND THE MONEY (Y/N)? *N*

BUDGET: $48653 . . .

ELECTIONS!!!

IT'S YOU AGAINST THE OLD DOGCATCHER.

VOTES:

FOR YOU: 855

FOR DOGCATCHER: 1145

WELL, IT LOOKS LIKE YOU LOST. BETTER LUCK NEXT TIME.

YOU HAD $33234 LEFT.

PLAY AGAIN (Y/N)? *N*

THANKS FOR PLAYING.

Appendix I: Quick Reference Guide

Here's a list of some of the features that commonly vary in different types of home computers. If you forget how to clear the screen, for instance (or if you're trying to translate a program from one computer to another), check this guide.

To Erase Letters One at a Time.

Apple: Use the left arrow key to back up the cursor. Make a correction when the cursor is positioned on the mistake. Use the space bar to erase. Use the right arrow key to move the cursor right without erasing.

Atari: Use the DELETE/BACK S key

Commodore: Use the INST/DEL key

TRS-80: Use the left arrow key ←

Texas Instruments: Hold the FCTN key and press S to back up the cursor to the position where you can correct the mistake. Use the space bar to erase. FCTN D moves the cursor right.

Timex Sinclair: Use SHIFT Ø

To Clear the Screen (In Immediate Mode).

Apple: Press ESC SHIFT @

Atari: Press SHIFT CLEAR/ <

Commodore: Press SHIFT CLR/HOME

TRS-80: Press CLEAR

Texas Instruments: Type CALL CLEAR

Timex Sinclair: Press V (for CLS)

To Clear the Screen (In a Program Line).

Apple: 1Ø HOME

Atari: 1Ø GR.Ø

or 1Ø PRINT "ESC CTRL CLEAR"

Commodore: You type: 1Ø PRINT "SHIFT CLR/HOME"
which appears on the screen as:
1Ø PRINT "♥"

TRS-80: 1Ø CLS
Texas Instruments: 1Ø CALL CLEAR
Timex Sinclair: 1Ø CLS

To Break into an Infinite Loop.

Apple: Hold down the CTRL key and press C
Atari
TRS-80 } Press BREAK
Commodore: Press RUN/STOP
Texas Instruments: Press FCTN 4
Timex Sinclair: Computer will stop when screen is full. (You may also press SPACE ENTER)

To Break into a Program at an Input Line.

Apple: Press CTRL C RETURN
Atari
TRS-80 } Press BREAK
Commodore VIC & 64: Press RUN/STOP with RESTORE
Commodore Pet: Press RUN/STOP and RETURN
Texas Instruments: Press FCTN 4
Timex Sinclair: Press SHIFT A ENTER (or SHIFT Ø SHIFT A ENTER)

To Stop or Slow Down a Scrolling Screen.

Apple: Hold down CTRL and type S to interrupt scrolling. Hit any key to continue.

Atari: Type CTRL 1 to interrupt scrolling and to start it up again.

TRS-80: Hold down SHIFT and type @ to interrupt scrolling. Press any key to continue.

Commodore: Holding down CTRL on the VIC makes the screen scroll more slowly. On the PET you must press RUN/STOP to interrupt scrolling; then type CONT to continue. (You may also do this on the VIC.)

Texas Instruments: Scrolls very slowly; freezing not necessary.

Timex Sinclair: Stops scrolling when screen is full.

To Make the Computer Pick a Random Number.

For a random number from 1 to 100:

Apple
Atari   R=INT(RND(1)*100)+1
Commodore

TRS-80: RANDOM:R=RND(100)

Texas Instruments
                LET R=INT(RND*100)+1
Timex Sinclair

For a random number between any high number (H) and any low number (L):

Apple
Atari   R=INT(RND(1)*(H−L+1))+L
Commodore

TRS-80: RANDOM:R=RND(H−L+1)+L−1

Texas Instruments
                LET R=INT(RND*(H−L+1))+L
Timex Sinclair

Appendix II: Troubleshooting

When your program doesn't work the way you want it to, the first step is to type **LIST**. If the computer tells you **SYNTAX ERROR IN 1Ø**, then type **LIST 1Ø**. *Note:* If your TRS-80 Model I or III tells you **SYNTAX ERROR IN 1Ø** it will also put you into Edit mode. For more about this, see Appendix III.

If you don't know exactly where the error is, then list a few lines at a time, like this:

    🍎 ℂ **TRS TI**   LIST Ø–5Ø

               or

        🏹 LIST Ø,5Ø

to list every line from 0 to 50.

Here are some things to check for:
- Did you misspell a keyword?
    - *Wrong:*   1Ø PRIMT 2+2
    - *Right:*   1Ø PRINT 2+2
- Did you type a O for a Ø, or vice versa?
    - *Wrong:*   10 GØTØ 20
    - *Right:*   1Ø GOTO 2Ø
- Did you put your quotes in the wrong place?
    - *Wrong:*   1Ø PRINT "HELLO N$"
    - *Right:*   1Ø PRINT "HELLO ";N$
- Did you forget to type `RETURN` (or `ENTER`) before starting a new line in the program? This is a very common mistake, especially when the cursor has automatically jumped to the beginning of a line on the screen. It's sometimes hard to see this mistake because when you **LIST** the whole program it looks okay. But when you tell the computer to **LIST 1Ø,** for instance, it prints:

        1Ø PRINT "HELLO, HOW ARE YOU?"

        2Ø GOTO 1Ø

In that case the computer doesn't know that 20 is supposed to be a new line; it thinks line 20 is part of line 10 and doesn't know what to do with it. You must remember that just putting the cursor on the left side of the screen doesn't start a new program line. You must press `RETURN` (or `ENTER`) to tell the computer "That's the end of line 10 — now start line 20."

To correct this mistake, retype both lines, and remember to press RETURN at the end of line 10 (and at the end of line 20).

• Did you forget to type **NEW** before you started your new program? If so, you'll see some lines from your old program mixed up with your new program confusing things. To fix this you'll have to erase all the old lines (by typing each line number and pressing RETURN).

Note: On the Apple and TRS-80 you can delete whole blocks of a program.

     On the Apple type **DEL 1Ø,5Ø**.

TRS   On the TRS-80 type **DELETE 1Ø–5Ø**.

          That will erase every line starting with line 10 and ending with line 50.

• Did you use the wrong number of quotes or the wrong number of parentheses? Remember, they come in pairs. If you count the quotation marks or parentheses in one line and come out with an odd number, something's wrong.

     Wrong: 1Ø PRINT "THE ANSWER IS ";N;APPLES"

      Right: 1Ø PRINT "THE ANSWER IS ";N;" APPLES."

     Wrong: 1Ø R=INT(RND(1) * (H−L+1) + L

      Right: 1Ø R=INT(RND(1) * (H−L+1)) + L

• Did you put a space in the wrong place, or leave out a space where there should be one?

     Wrong: 1Ø DATA CAT, DOG, HORSE, COW

      Right: 1Ø DATA CAT,DOG,HORSE,COW

     Wrong: 1Ø IF A$=" YES" THEN GOTO 5Ø

      Right: 1Ø IF A$="YES" THEN GOTO 5Ø

Some computers won't let you put a space in the word **GOTO**. Others don't care if you type **GO TO**.

Some computers won't let you type expressions like **RND (1)** — with a space before the **(1)** — instead of **RND(1)**.

• Did you forget to put a colon between two commands in one line?

     Wrong: 1Ø PRINT "HI" PRINT "HO"

      Right: 1Ø PRINT "HI":PRINT "HO"

> *Wrong:*   1Ø IF A<>B THEN PRINT "WRONG" GOTO 3Ø
>
> *Right:*   1Ø IF A<>B THEN PRINT "WRONG":GOTO 3Ø

TI T/S   *Remember:* If you have a TI or a Timex Sinclair, you may not put two statements in one line.

- Did you forget to put your strings inside quotation marks?

> *Wrong:*   1Ø IF A$=CAT THEN PRINT "MEOW"
>
> *Right:*   1Ø IF A$="CAT" THEN PRINT "MEOW"

- Did you forget that some key words come in pairs?

> **THEN** must go with **IF**
>
> **NEXT** must go with **FOR**
>
> **RETURN** must go with **GOSUB** (and you usually must have an **END** in your program)
>
> **DATA** must go with **READ**

- Did you accidentally type a hidden control character that you can't see? This is practically an impossible error to detect — so if the computer keeps telling you **SYNTAX ERROR** but you can't figure out what your error is, just try retyping the whole line carefully. Sometimes that will solve the problem when nothing else seems to work.

- Did you try to put too much in one program line? On most computers 255 characters is the limit for one line of a BASIC program.

C=   On the VIC a program line can be no more than 88 characters long. (That's 4 lines on the TV screen.)

TI   The TI will only allow you to type 4 screen lines in one program line.

Λ   The Atari will buzz when you try to make your program line too long.

Appendix III: Editing Your Mistakes

On almost any program you type, you will make mistakes. The least complicated way to fix your mistakes is to press RETURN or ENTER, type the whole line over again, beginning with the line number, and press RETURN (or ENTER) again. That works on every computer. It will erase the line that had the mistake and put the new line in its place.

Sometimes, though, especially if your line is long, you really don't want to have to retype the whole thing. So here's a quick rundown on how to use the editing functions on your computer to let you correct mistakes without retyping whole lines.

Editing on the Apple

On the Apple it's easy to edit a mistake in a line if you catch it before you hit RETURN. Just use the left arrow key to move back to your mistake. Then you can use the right arrow key to get back to the end of the line without retyping.

If you find your mistake after you've hit RETURN and you don't want to retype the line, you can use the ESC key to put you in Edit mode. Here's what you should do:

1. First, press ESC. Then press the letter I to move you up to the line where you see the mistake. (After you press ESC once, you don't have to press it again to keep moving the cursor. Every time you press I the cursor will move up one more line.)

2. When the cursor is on the line you want, then press the J key to put it on the first number in the line. *This is very important. If you don't get the cursor over the first number, the correction will not get made.*

3. Use the right arrow key to move the cursor to the mistake. Then correct the mistake. If you have more than one mistake in the line, correct them all as you go along.

4. Continue pressing the right arrow key (on the Apple II+, this is most easily done by using REPT) until the cursor comes to the end of the program line. (That means everything in line 10, for example, not just everything on one line of the screen.) If you don't do this, the computer will erase the last part of the line.

5. Then press RETURN to enter your correction in the memory of the computer.

Note: Once you press ESC you are in Edit mode. You may continue pressing I, J, K, or M to move the cursor. Pressing any other key (or even pressing ESC a second time) turns I, J, K, and M back to ordinary typing keys.

The right arrow key and ESC K both move the cursor to the right. The difference is this: When the right arrow key sends the cursor over a letter, it is recopying the letter into the computer's memory. When you use ESC K to move the cursor over a letter, it tells the computer to ignore that letter.

You may use the Edit mode on a line you've just finished typing, or after you tell the computer to LIST the line. However, when the computer lists the line, it may print it on the screen with spaces that aren't actually part of the line. Example:

You type:

```
1Ø PRINT "HELLO, MY NAME IS APPLE COMPY
UTER." RETURN
LIST RETURN
```

The computer prints:

```
        1Ø PRINT "HELLO, MY NAME IS APPL
                E COMPYUTER."
```

The listing shows 12 extra spaces between the L and E in APPLE. This makes it more complicated to use the Edit function. If you use the right arrow key to move the cursor over those 12 spaces, you are actually putting extra spaces into your program. So you will have to switch from the right arrow key to ESC K in order to move the cursor over those 12 spaces.

One way around this is to type POKE 33,33 RETURN *before* you type LIST. The line(s) will then appear without those extra spaces. When you finish your editing (after you press RETURN), then type TEXT RETURN before you go on to do anything else.

Editing on the Atari

When you make a typing mistake on the Atari, it immediately tells you so, like this:

You type: 1Ø PRIMT "HI"

The Atari prints: 1Ø ERROR-PRIMT [••]HI"

(The computer will highlight your mistake by printing a white box after it.)

Once you have made that error, the word ERROR becomes part of line 10. If you now type LIST 1Ø, the Atari repeats:

1Ø ERROR-PRIMT [••]HI"

If you want to correct that error using the editing functions on the Atari, you can do this:

1. Use the cursor arrow keys (with the CTRL key) to move the cursor to the beginning of line 10 and on to just after the last letter of ERROR.

2. Erase the word ERROR, using the DELETE key, while holding CTRL.

3. Use the right cursor arrow key to put the cursor over the M. Type N to spell the word correctly.

4. Continue moving the cursor right to the white box. Retype the character inside the box correctly.

5. Press RETURN to enter your correction into the memory of the computer.

This is a rather involved process, so for simple corrections like this one, you'll probably usually find it easier to retype the line from the beginning, starting with the line number. Just remember, you must always press RETURN when you finish your corrections in order to enter them into the computer's memory.

Editing on the Commodore

Editing mistakes on the VIC, 64, or the PET is very simple. All you have to do is use the cursor arrow keys to move the cursor to the mistake, wherever it is on the screen. Then you correct the mistake and press RETURN.

Here are a few examples of how you might correct misspellings:

Mistake: PRIMT

Use the cursor arrow keys to place the cursor directly over the M. Then type N and press RETURN.

Mistake: PRINIT

Place the cursor over the T. Press the INST/DEL key. This will erase the I.

Mistake: PRNT

Place the cursor over the **N**. Hold the [SHIFT] key and press the [INST/DEL] key. This will open up a space before the **N**, with the cursor now on top of the space. Type the missing **I** in the space and press [RETURN].

Notice that when using the [INST/DEL] key to make corrections, you should position the cursor just *after* the mistake. When you want to change one letter into another, put the cursor directly over the mistake, and type the new letter.

And don't forget to press [RETURN] after you've made your correction. [RETURN] is what tells the computer to remember the correction. You can correct more than one mistake in a single program line before you press [RETURN]. (For example, if you have two mistakes in line 10, correct one, move the cursor, correct the second, then press [RETURN]). But you must press [RETURN] before going on to edit a new line.

Possible problem: If you type a quote mark like this " and then try to use the cursor arrow or [INST/DEL] keys, you will start getting funny little reversed characters on the screen. That's because the computer thinks you are telling it to print the cursor arrow key instead of moving the cursor immediately.

If you need to type a quotation mark, then continue making corrections, press [RETURN] after you type the quotation. Then move the cursor back up again to make the rest of your corrections.

Example:

    Mistake: **PRINT HEELLO"**

1. Move the cursor to the space after the **T**.
2. Type the quotation mark.
3. Press [RETURN].
4. Move the cursor back up to the second **E**.
5. Press [INST/DEL] to erase the extra **E**.
6. Press [RETURN].

Editing on the TI 99/4A

Imagine that you have typed a line full of mistakes, such as this:

    1Ø PRUNNT "HELO"XXX

Here's how you can fix it, using the Edit mode on your computer.

1. First, type EDIT 1Ø and press ENTER. Line 10 should reappear with the cursor on the first character after the number 10, like this:

    10 P̄RUNNT "HELO"XXX

2. Hold the FCTN key and type D to move the cursor over to the U. Type I to change the U into an I.

3. To wipe out a letter, use FCTN 1. In this line you want to delete the extra N, so move the cursor right again until it is on top of the N. Then type FCTN 1 to erase the N.

4. To insert a letter, type FCTN 2. You want to insert an extra L in "HELO", so move the cursor over to the L. Then type FCTN 2, and type L.

Note: Once you type FCTN 2, the computer will keep on inserting until you press FCTN again with another key.

5. To erase the extra X's, move the cursor right with FCTN D. Then erase with the space bar.

6. Press ENTER when you have finished making corrections, to enter the new line into the computer's memory.

Editing on TRS-80 (Models I & III)

On the TRS-80 Models I and III when you try to run a program with an error in any line, the computer will automatically put you in Edit mode as soon as it comes to the error. When you are in Edit mode, the computer is waiting to get your instructions on how to correct the mistake(s). In Edit mode your computer no longer behaves like a typewriter. It is now a correcting machine. This section will explain some of the special orders you may use in the Edit mode.

If you spot the error first and you want to make the computer go into Edit mode, you type EDIT and the line number, such as EDIT 1Ø.

When you go into Edit mode, you will see the line number appear on the screen, followed by the cursor. After that, each time you press the space bar, one more character from your line will appear on the screen. Here's an example of a line with some common errors, and instructions on editing them:

1Ø PRUNTT "HELO"XXXXXXX

In that line, you want to: 1) change the U to I; 2) delete the extra T; 3) insert L in HELO; and 4) get rid of all those X's at the end. Here's how to do each of those things. (If you want to practice using the Edit mode, type that line full of mistakes, press ENTER, then follow these directions):

1. First type EDIT 1Ø and press ENTER. The number 10 should appear, followed by the cursor.

2. Type L (for List). This makes the whole line, mistakes and all, reappear. Underneath it you should again see the line number 10 and the cursor.

3. When you are in Edit mode, you use the space bar to move the cursor to the right and use the left arrow key to move the cursor to the left. Each time you press the space bar, one more character in your messed-up line will appear. If you accidentally space past the mistake, use the left arrow key to back up.

Press the space bar until you see this:

1Ø PR

The cursor is now under the first mistake (the U), but you can't see the U.

4. To change the last character, press C (for *Change*), then the new letter, I. Presto — the U becomes an I and appears in the correct space!

5. Move the cursor by pressing the space bar until the first T appears. In order to get rid of the next character — the extra T — type D (for *Delete*), and the T is erased. The T appears inside exclamation points like this:

1Ø PRINT!T!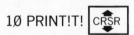

The exclamation points are just there to show you that you've erased the T. They won't stay there. Anything you see inside those exclamation points will disappear when you list the line again.

6. Space the cursor over to the L. Press I for *Insert*). Type L, and you now have HELLO spelled correctly.

7. Unfortunately, the computer has no way of knowing that you were only going to insert one L. If you type anything else now, it will keep on insert-

ing. So, for example, if you press the space bar, hoping to see the O, the computer will insert a space in the word: "HELL O".

In order to get out of insert mode, you must press SHIFT ↑ .

8. Now the only thing left to do is to knock off all those extra X's. So move the cursor over to just after the last quote mark.

9. Then type H (for *Hack*), and the rest of the line is erased.

10. To record your changes, press ENTER . That takes you out of Edit mode.

11. If you want to be sure everything was corrected, type LIST 1Ø. You should then see the line in its final correct form:

       1Ø PRINT "HELLO"

A few other commands you might find useful in Edit mode are these:

Q (for *Quit*) is what you type if you've made some corrections, then change your mind about all of them. Q takes you out of Edit mode and leaves your program line as it was before you started making changes.

Typing SB will search for the letter B, and move the cursor automatically to the first B in the line. 2SB will search for the second B, 3SB, for the third B, etc. (This may also be done with any other character besides B, of course.)

Handy Reference Guide to Control Characters in TRS-80 Edit Mode:

Space bar: Move cursor one space to right and show the character just before the cursor.

Left arrow key: Back up the cursor.

C: Change one character into another.

D: Delete or erase a character.

I: Insert one or more characters.

SHIFT ↑ :   Stop inserting; go back to regular Edit mode.

H: Hack, or chop off everything from there to the end of the line.

S: Search.

Q: Quit.

L: List.

Appendix IV: What Is a Computer?

We've put this section near the end of the book because it's a lot easier to understand how a computer works after you've played around with one for a while. Also, you really don't need to know about what goes on inside the computer to be able to use it. You can write perfectly good programs without knowing anything about bits and bytes or ROM and RAM. But most people who start fooling around with computers eventually want to learn something more about what makes them compute. So if you're curious — read on.

The word used to describe the machinery that makes up your computer and the other parts that connect to it is "hardware." In order to use a computer you need three main pieces of hardware: (1) An *input* device; (2) The *central processing unit*; (CPU) (3) An *output* device.

The input device lets you put information into the computer. When you write a program, the input device you use is the *keyboard*. Any time you press a key you are putting one piece of information into the computer. Other examples of input devices your computer may or may not have are: tape recorder/player with tapes, disk drive with disks, joystick or paddles, light pen, and touch-sensitive screen.

People are now trying to perfect computers that will accept voice input, so that you can put information in just by saying it.

All of these devices let you send some kind of signal into the computer. The place where they send the input is the *CPU,* the central processing unit. This is the "brains" of the computer, the part that makes it work. (You probably can't see the CPU on your computer, because it's inside the case, as your brain is inside your head. On most personal computers the CPU and the keyboard are parts of the same package.)

Think about your own body. You can get input through your eyes, ears, nose, mouth, or skin. But you don't know what to do with that input until your brain tells you. If you didn't have a brain, you wouldn't know that a fire was hot. You would just leave your hand in a flame until it was burned to a crisp. It is your brain that figures out FIRE means HOT means HURT means GET AWAY.

The CPU inside the computer is not made of brain cells. It's made mostly of *silicon* — the main ingredient in common sand (more about that later). And it's not nearly as smart as your brain. But it has much the same job — to figure out what to do with the information that gets sent to it as input and then to translate that information into useful output.

The *output* device used by most home computers is the TV screen. Actually, it doesn't have to be a TV set, and some more accurate computer names for this device are: video display terminal (VDT), cathode ray tube (CRT), or monitor.

Other types of output devices are printers (to put your output on paper) and speakers (to make sound output). Output can also be sent to various types of machines, which are usually hooked up to special-purpose computers such as those in factories or laboratories. Robots in factories, for example, are output devices whose movements are controlled by computers.

You can also make your computer a two-way communicator — sending output and receiving input to and from faraway places — with a device called a *modem*. A modem is a connection that allows your computer to use the telephone lines to "talk" to other computers. If you and your friend both have modems on your computers, you can transmit your programs back and forth over the phone lines.

Probably the most exciting use of the modem allows your computer to tap into the resources of much larger collections of information on other computers. Through this communication hookup, your computer can locate for you facts on the latest medical discoveries, political news, or sports scores. It can allow you to browse through catalogs, order, and pay for items without ever leaving your home or taking out your wallet.

Your computer's input can come from a data base thousands of miles away or from its own keyboard. No matter where the input starts, it's the output, obviously, that makes the computer useful to people. You must be able to see, hear, or feel the messages the computer is sending if they're going to do you any good. Your brain can tell you a fire is hot, but knowing that fact won't help you if your brain doesn't also get the message to your muscles to take your hand away. That final effect — the way the computer responds after processing the input — is the output.

So how does the computer manage to process all these input messages into usable output? It does this by breaking down complicated messages into simpler ones so that it can rearrange them. First it painstakingly translates each item of input into a pattern of electrical impulses — using a code made up of patterns of 1's and 0's. These 1's and 0's represent whether individual tiny electrical switches inside the computer are on (1) or off (0). Early computers (back around the 1950s) used a system of vacuum tubes to transmit on/off information. Sometimes filling whole rooms, those first computers were *much* larger machines than today's microcomputers, although they were often much less powerful in terms of what they could do. As time went on, scientists developed ways to get the same (or a better) effect with much smaller electronic devices. And now thousands of "on/off switches" can be packed onto a tiny square or "chip" of silicon in what is called an *integrated circuit*. You can't tell by looking at a silicon chip how it works, because its information comes in the form of invisible electrical or magnetic signals, and because the whole thing is so tiny.

Though you can't see what the chips are doing, you can — if you have a computer like an Apple, which makes it easy for you to look inside the cover — open up the case and see how the chips are installed. The actual chips are inside all those little black boxes, which are connected together by being plugged into the *circuit boards*. The circuit boards are the large flat green rectangles with silvery tracings. These transmit the electrical signals through the computer.

If you could see what was going on inside a chip, you would see something like thousands and thousands of tiny switches being turned on and off. The switches work much the same way as an electric light switch. When you push up on a wall switch, it lets in the electric current, and the light comes on. When you push the switch down, the current is stopped and the light goes off. The switches inside a computer, of course, do not look like electric light switches.

But they do turn "on" or "off" to let electricity in or keep it out, and those on/off patterns make up the language of the computer.

In the language of mathematics, we say that computers use *binary* code. That means that every message you send the computer is eventually translated into a 0 (representing off) or a 1 (representing on). Each 0 and 1 is called a BInary digiT, which is abbreviated to the word *bit*. Bits are combined into groups of 8, and each eight-bit group is called a *byte*.

Here's an example of how bits combine into bytes to stand for our letters and numbers. (You'll notice that only 7 bits are actually used in the code. The eighth bit is not a part of the code but is used to represent other information that tells the computer how to carry out its operations.)

Number	Binary Code	Letter	Binary Code
0	0000000	A	1000001
1	0000001	B	1000010
2	0000010	C	1000011
3	0000011	D	1000100
4	0000100	E	1000101
5	0000101		

When you press an A on the keyboard, that keystroke is translated into the series of 1's and 0's that you see above. Those 1's and 0's cause the tiny switches inside the CPU to go on and off in a pattern that ultimately transmits a signal to the video display. On the monitor that signal is transformed to a shape we recognize as the letter A. (These patterns of 0's and 1's to represent letters and numbers are known as the ASCII code — or American Standard Code for Information Interchange. This code is used to form the machine language, or the lowest level language on the computer. Inside your computer a high-level language such as BASIC gets translated into this low-level machine language.)

With such a simple idea behind it all, a computer can do so many seemingly complicated things for two reasons:

1. It has a very large number of switches that can produce a great many different patterns.

2. It can perform its switching operations incredibly fast. The most powerful computers can do millions of calculations per second. In a matter of minutes computers can figure problems that would take a person more than a lifetime to do with a pencil and paper.

But when it seems that a computer is performing miracles, remember that its only real miracles are its size (a lot of switches compressed into a very small space) and its speed. At the bottom of it all, everything is still reduced to those 1's and 0's.

And when you think about how that works, you may understand why you have to spell everything out for the computer in such painstakingly simple terms. (IF A=B THEN PRINT "YES.") Everything you want a computer to do must be translated into something that can be answered either yes or no.

That's why a computer is good at solving problems that have only one right answer ("What is 2 + 2?"). Trouble often begins when people start expecting the computer to give them answers to questions like "What should we do to solve the economic problems of our government?" There are so many possible answers to that question that probably no two computer programs would give you the same solution.

A few more terms you should know if you want to consider yourself "computer literate" are ROM, RAM, and K (for Kilobyte). These all have to do with the *memory* of your computer.

ROM stands for Read Only Memory. This is the memory that stays inside your computer when you turn it off. It is permanently programmed into the computer by the people who built it. ROM is made up of the aspects that you always want to work the same way when you use the computer. For example, you don't want to have to learn a different system for loading a program every time you turn on your computer. So the information that tells the computer "This is how you take a program from the disk and get it running" is a part of

ROM. If your computer automatically understands BASIC when you turn it on, then BASIC is part of the ROM of your computer.

Read Only Memory means that the computer can only read information out of it. You cannot change (or "write into") the information in ROM. For instance, you can't decide that you want to change the word PRINT to TYPE in your programs. PRINT, as the command to put information on the screen, is permanently part of the BASIC language in your computer, and there's nothing you can do to change that except build a new computer. Other examples of the ROM in your computer are the parts of the memory that tell the computer what to do when you turn on the switch, how to save information on disks or tapes, how to send a picture to the CRT, etc.

RAM, or Random Access Memory, is what you use when you write a program, or when you load a program for a tape or disk. When you type NEW, or put in another disk, or turn off the computer, everything in the RAM changes or disappears. The RAM allows you to add to and subtract from your programs and to use your computer for an infinite number of different programs at different times.

You will often see a computer's memory described in terms something like this: 16 K in RAM. That K stands for kilobyte(s). Kilo means 1000 — so a computer with 16 K in RAM can hold a program containing approximately 16,000 bytes. Since a byte is approximately equal to one English letter or number, you could type in about 16,000 characters before that computer ran out of memory space to store the program.

This has been a very quick and very general summary of how a computer works. You'll probably want to find other books and magazines to read more about the history, functions, and operations of the computer. Meanwhile, just as a check on *your* Random Access Memory, you might want to see how many of these terms you can remember after reading this section:

Hardware	Video display terminal (VDT)
Bit	Modem
Byte	RAM
Kilobyte	ROM

Input

CPU

Output

Cathode ray tube (CRT)

Monitor

Silicon chip

Circuit board

Binary code

Machine language

Index